FINDING GRACE

ALSO BY DONNA VanLIERE

FINDING GRACE

A True Story About
Losing Your Way in Life . . .
And Finding It Again

DONNA VanLIERE

ST. MARTIN'S PRESS ❦ New York

FINDING GRACE. Copyright © 2009 by Donna VanLiere. All rights reserved. Printed in the United States of America. For information, address St. Martin's Press, 175 Fifth Avenue, New York, N.Y. 10010.

www.stmartins.com

Design by Patrice Sheridan

LIBRARY OF CONGRESS CATALOGING-IN-PUBLICATION DATA

VanLiere, Donna, 1966–
    Finding Grace : a true story about losing your way in life . . . and finding it again / Donna VanLiere.—1st ed.
        p. cm.
    ISBN-13: 978-0-312-38054-0

    1. VanLiere, Donna, 1966–   2. VanLiere, Donna, 1966—Religion.
3. Grace (Theology)   4. Authors, American—21st century—Biography.   5. Adult child sexual abuse victims—Biography.   6. Infertility, Female—Patients—United States—Biography.   7. Adoptive parents—United States—Biography.
8. Life change events.   I. Title.
    PS3622.A66Z46 2009
    813'.6—dc22
    [B]

                                                                    2008043920

First Edition: April 2009

P1

For David and Vicki VanLiere,
who give it away

ACKNOWLEDGMENTS

Many thanks to . . .

Troy, who kept after me for years to write this book.

Gracie, Kate, and David for providing an endless supply of material, ideas and joy.

Jen at ZSH, who for several years asked, "So when do you want to talk about Grace?" And to both her and Esmond for keeping me on point when we did talk about it. Thank you both for continued enthusiasm, guidance, and friendship.

Jen E., who wanted to publish this book while chatting

at dinner. Without even reading a word she believed. Thank you, Jen, for always making each book better.

Sally, John, Matt, Tara, and the St. Martin's sales team, for boundless creativity, feedback, and belief.

Mom and Dad VL., and Lindsey Wolford (making a brief stopover from Ireland), who love spending time with the small people in our family.

David and Marilyn Knight, for the weekend at their home that got this book started.

Chris Carter and Anita Pringle, for reading an early version of the manuscript and providing input and encouragement.

Julie Cranston, Kathy Marlin, Rosie Mitchell, Renee Sly, Charity Compton, Sylvia Fitzgerald, Pam Dillon, Jamie Betts, Karen Parente, Carole Consiglio, and Robin Thomason, for your heart.

Joseph Cassell, for sharing his gift with an old friend.

And to the folks at Meridee's, who keep the coffee and pastries hot and fresh, and Graeme and staff at The Mercantile, who have let me work long after they've closed.

◆ ◆ ◆

P R E F A C E

IT'S COLD IN TENNESSEE TODAY. From my window I can
see the cows grazing in the pasture next door and our
dog's breath as she runs around our home. Although she
has plenty of space to roam she continues to run the same
pattern, creating a twelve-inch barren circular path around
the perimeter of the house that is peppered with holes
where she digs after moles. We try to explain that she
doesn't have to dig *that* far to get to the moles but she ig-
nores us. My husband cringes every time he sees the path
and the holes. I tell him not to look. He's throwing scraps
of insulation and wood out of our attic window; he and my
father-in-law have been banging and pounding for weeks
as they finish converting our attic space into an office. "So

you can write," my husband says. It's difficult to write with garbage flying past my window but, save the banging, it's quiet in the house so maybe I'll get a couple of hours to pluck a few letters from the alphabet and to arrange them into some sort of shape before company arrives. Our old college friend Bob will be visiting for a few days and I need to change the sheets and clean the bathroom. The dog's barking now—at the cows in the pasture next to us. The barking also drives my husband crazy. This day, the writing, the banging, the sailing debris, the cows, the moles, everything is so different from what I wanted as a child. It seems life rarely turns out the way we picture it, though.

I had a plan when I was little. As far as dreams went it was tidy and organized and well constructed. I used to watch the *Little Rascals* series after school and on the weekends I'd see reruns of *The Andy Griffith Show*, *I Love Lucy*, and countless old movies on Channel 43 out of Cleveland. I watched those shows and knew I wanted to be an actress and marry a guy who looked like those men in the movies with dark hair and blue eyes (I assumed; it *was* black-and-white TV), and I wanted to have three or four children. I envisioned a home like the ones I'd see in movies with a charming picket fence and blooming flowerbeds that wrapped around the house. Like all childlike plans I saw my husband loving his job, I was happy and fulfilled in my own, and my children were well behaved, healthy, and well adjusted. That was my dream. Not a lot of bells and whistles. In the grand scheme of things it was really very simple but no one told me then that in one moment life could blindside me and I'd never see it coming.

Someone early in our lives should tell us that we'll never make it to the end unscathed or pain free but I guess for centuries people have all thought the same thing about the next generation: "They'll figure it out." Many never figure it out, though. We just suck up the pain of the divorce, the rape, the abuse, the death, or the financial collapse and carry on the best we know how, hobbling along toward the finish line. It seems that God, or at the very least an angel, should appear at life-altering moments to offer guidance for the life that's now ours but that doesn't happen. We're left to figure out things on our own.

We hope for a life that exceeds our dreams, and when those dreams collapse we simply wish for a soft wing of hope, but instead we get life in a culture of ungrace. I know that's not a word but it works here. (Disgrace doesn't apply since it's a different word altogether and nongrace just doesn't "sound" as good.) If you don't know what ungrace is, just hop on the interstate at rush hour, or watch how quickly Hollywood turns on a star who doesn't shine like he once did at the box office, or sit in a room full of lawyers at divorce proceedings. Ungrace pulsates in our workplaces, our communities, and in the media, and tells us that regardless of what has happened we must do better, look better, and make ourselves better. But to love and accept someone regardless of their flaws and failures is a breath of hope in a harsh, finger-wagging world. That is an undeserved gift, which is life itself. That's grace.

The following pages are part of my story. If I share these experiences in a way that breathes shape and color into them perhaps you'll recognize part of your own life as well. Samuel Johnson said that people need more to be reminded than to be instructed. Sometimes we need to be reminded of why we're here, that we are valued and loved, and at the end of the pain there are still deeper and higher dreams to discover. This is the story of how I finally figured that out.

O N E

Lord, I suffer much. I cannot tell You what goes on inside of me, I cannot hide from You these dark battles, the deep despair. When God breathes on man, He opens his inner being and sees deeply within it.

—VICTOR HUGO, FRENCH POET AND NOVELIST

WE MOVED TO OUR HOME in Medina, Ohio, in the spring of 1970, when I was three. My brother, Brian, was seven and got his own room, the green one with the short, shaggy dark green carpet. I shared a room with my sister Mary Jo (we call her Josie . . . like Jocie, not Jozey), who is nearly ten years older than me. We got the baby-aspirin-orange room with the orange shag carpet, and my parents got the all-purple room. The family room was pink, the living room blue, and the kitchen had bluish-green-patterned indoor/outdoor carpeting and avocado appliances. The house screamed 1960s.

There were a few homes on our road but it was mostly farmland. Our split-level house had a long, blacktop driveway, huge front lawn, brick front, a white barn in the back that would hold my dad's tractors and gardening equipment, and over an acre of land behind the barn for a garden that could feed most of Medina County (my parents never believed in small gardens). Our neighbor Mr. Lake also had a garden behind his barn. Bud Lake had a round chest that was slick as a watermelon. It actually glistened on hot summer days when he worked outside. When we met Mr. Lake for the first time I whispered to my mother, "That man doesn't have any hair on his chest." She tried to shush me but I was three and lacked whispering skills. Mr. Lake believed in using manure for fertilizer. He'd haul in a huge load from somewhere and let it percolate inside his barn before he used it. His garden always smelled crappy, but it was lovely.

A dairy was just up the street and Mr. Lake walked to work there every morning with his lunch pail in hand. Sometimes (but not nearly enough) he'd bring home a package of ice-cream bars and hand them to me. Life couldn't get any better than on those free ice-cream-bar days. One morning as I played in the driveway I was talking to myself, weaving together an outlandish tale full of colorful characters, intrigue, and drama. I froze when I saw Mr. Lake peering from behind one of his trees, listening to me. "Go on," he said. "I can't wait to hear what happens." Stage fright hit me and I couldn't utter another word. I ran toward our garage door and heard Mr. Lake laughing from his yard.

Across the road was a pasture full of cows for the dairy and right next to us was an old farmhouse where our other neighbors lived. For the sake of this story I'll just call them the "Taylors." Theirs was not a charming farmhouse in any way. The exterior hadn't been painted in years and what was left of the old paint fell like curly, white pencil shavings around the house. A distinct odor of aged, rotting wood, cigarettes, and filth met you before stepping onto the porch. My mother was and is a no-nonsense woman. She and my father both grew up in east Tennessee working on farms that fed fifteen children in my father's family and five in my mother's. My dad's oldest sibling, my Aunt Stella, was born the same year as my maternal grandmother, Mary Hurley. As Grandma Hurley grew, got married, and began having children of her own, my paternal grandmother was *still* giving birth to her fifteen children. When she died in 1972, her death certificate claimed she was *just worn out*.

My mother was always very practical (as I write this sitting at a plastic folding table I know the apple hasn't fallen too far from the tree) and called things as she saw them. On more than one occasion I remember her looking at our neighbor's home and saying, "Move next to a dump and you live next to trash." I didn't know what she meant.

When we moved to Medina my mom worked at the latex factory, the flower container factory, and then later, the box factory. (My sister eventually worked at the pickle factory.) My mother settled on cleaning homes as a business because she could set her own hours and be home when we got off the school bus in the afternoon. My dad worked second shift in one of the steel mills in Cleveland, the same one he'd worked in since he moved to Ohio in 1955 and ultimately retired from forty years later. At night I'd fall asleep in my mother's bed and when my dad got home in the early morning hours he would carry me to my orange room. I never remembered a thing.

After I learned to read I would crawl into bed with my mom and read *her* stories. Mother would come home from the factory and make dinner for my siblings and me, maybe do a load of laundry, or scrub a spot on the indoor/outdoor kitchen carpet before turning in each night. I'd riffle through my books or the ones we'd picked up at the library and read one after the other out loud to my mother as she fell asleep. I'd look over at her and think, "Why are you so tired?" I'd read till I got sleepy and then turn out the light, thinking about new books to bring home.

The Franklin Sylvester Library was just off the square in Medina. I would crawl on the floor between the stacks of books in the children's section in search of two or three new ones to take home. Long before I could read I loved to flip through the pages of a book and look at the pictures. The individual volumes in the Childcraft books that still stand on my parents' shelves reveal my scribbling then as I learned my ABCs and my failed attempts to write my name (the Ns are still backward). One winter's night my mother bundled me up to take books back to the library. I set three books on top of the car while I put on my boots but forgot them as I climbed into my seat. When we got to the library I searched the car for the books, thinking I'd left them at home. Mother discovered one of the books still sitting on top of the car; the other two had no doubt come to an ugly ending somewhere along the route. I was petrified as we walked into the library, so frightened that the lady behind the desk would take away our library card or worse yet, that she'd ban me from stepping foot inside the library again. I don't remember if my mother paid for the books or if the woman behind the desk was just gracious to an absent-minded child but we left that evening after checking out two new books. We went home and had a piece of chocolate cake. There was always dessert in my mother's kitchen. My mother was and still is an amazing cook. She had dinner on the table every night. A little neighbor girl up the road timed her visits to our house at dinnertime and was always ecstatic when my mom asked if she wanted to stay for dinner. "Oh, is it dinnertime? I guess I could stay," she'd say, filling her plate. She was accustomed to Ramen noodles or a cold sandwich and was just beside herself when my mother put mashed potatoes, green beans, corn, coleslaw, corn bread, and baked chicken on the table. My mother was raised on a Southern farm and in the South you do not have a meal unless there are at least three vegetables on the table. That's the rule. We had a little dog named Jack; he was part Pekingese and part Pomeranian, not a good mix for children. He was high strung and temperamental and my arms still bear scars from more than one run-in with him. After any meal we could drop a piece of food into his dish, *plink, plunk,* and he'd come tearing through the house. My mother took him to the joint vocational school to get his hair cut once and the students shaved him bald except for the fur on his head. He looked like a Dr. Seuss cartoon animal and was so ashamed that he came home and hid under the drum table in the corner of the blue living room. One

morning my mother caught him taking his daily constitu-
tion in her bedroom and she was so angry that she picked
him up and shook him. Tiny poop shot out like torpedoes
onto the purple carpet and she ran for the door with Jack
hanging like a sack of potatoes in front of her. That was
high comedy for a kid and I fell down laughing. My mother
didn't. Jack was mean, but I loved him; he was a constant
playmate. Give me a few Barbies, baby dolls, and Jack, and
I was set for the day. I was a happy kid.

George and Tess Taylor lived next door to us with
their five children, all of whom were much older than me
except Tom, who was my age. Sometime after our move I
walked with my mother across the field that divided our
homes and met the Taylors. Tom was in the yard playing
with the family's shaggy, bounding yellow dog. "I'm Tom,"
he said, pounding the dog's side. "And this is Ziggy, the
butt-sniffing dog." He smacked the dog's muzzle back and
forth and took off running. Ziggy chased after him and
pushed his snoot into Tom's rear end, hoisting him into
the air. "That's why we call him a butt sniffer," Tom yelled,
laughing.

"Stop doing that to that dog," Tess said, taking a drag
off her cigarette. "You'll turn him mean." Tess had a mess of
reddish-orange hair and the longest toenails I'd ever seen in

my life. She was wearing sandals (no way those nails could fit inside a shoe) and an orange jumpsuit with a belt that tied in the front. Although it was the seventies I can proudly say that my mother never owned a polyester jumpsuit. Tess was down to earth and warm, and called me "Sugar Pop" most of the time.

Tom had dark hair and eyes like his dad, his brother Kevin, and his sister Cindy, who had enormous breasts. Of course the hugeness was accentuated by the lack of bra she often excluded. As Tom and I played in the backyard one day he stopped, doubled over, and vomited right on his feet. I ran to the house to find Cindy. She was on the front porch, ironing. Her breasts swayed from side to side as she moved the iron back and forth over a shirt. "Tom just puked," I said.

"He did what?"

I couldn't remember the other word for puke. My mind raced: *It was a grown-up word, what did it start with? Hurry. Hurry. Oh, I got nothing.* "He just opened his mouth and all sorts of chunks flew out," I said. She jumped off the porch and I couldn't believe that whatever was under her T-shirt was actually attached to her body. She helped Tom to the porch and went back to her ironing. I watched in silence then finally asked, "Do you have water balloons under there?" She reared back her head and laughed. I didn't know if that was a yes or no.

I don't know where George worked and I don't think Tess did anything more than smoke cigarettes and paint her toenails. I'd often catch her slathering on a new coat of candy-apple red when I'd be playing at their house. I'd look down at those ugly, glistening nails when she was finished and wonder if she took the skin off George's shins in bed each evening. These were the things that kept me up at night. That, and why Tarzan didn't have a beard.

I never really got to know the oldest siblings, Marty and Tabitha. They weren't interested in me and I don't remember having a conversation with them. Kevin was in the middle: younger than Cindy and older than Tom, he had long, greasy hair and a dour personality. "There's just something about that kid that I don't like," my mother said time and again. I didn't like him, either, but I didn't know why. He'd never done anything to me, and like his older siblings he never paid attention to me, but I hated it when he called Tom a little shit or piss head and I wondered why George or Tess didn't make him stop. Cindy was definitely my favorite of Tom's siblings. She gave me a piece of candy any time I asked for it and that made her tops in my book. After awhile I learned to ignore her great, heaving breasts and love her for the buxom candy dispenser that she was.

Tom was either at my house in our giant sandbox making what he called "butt butt trails" or I was crossing through the field to play with him and Ziggy. My mother was at the grocery store one afternoon when Tom came over to play. We wandered into the barn, a place my mother had told me countless times I "had no business being in," and I climbed on top of a huge oil barrel with a lid. I was pretending to be a bus driver when my weight collapsed the outer rim of the lid and my leg fell down into the barrel. I screamed as sharp metal broke the skin on my thigh, just above my knee, and my leg was immersed in oil. To this day I don't know why my dad had a huge barrel of oil inside the barn but he did and I took a bath in it. I tried to pull myself out but couldn't get a good grip; my hands were too slippery. Tom yanked on my arms till I was able to hoist myself up and over the rim.

A dark mixture of oil and blood streamed down my leg and I grabbed one of my dad's barn rags to wipe it off. Tom found a rag and began wiping as well. I was a bloody, oily mess and my mother wasn't home. I sat on the barn floor and pressed the oily rag onto the cut, waiting for it to stop bleeding but it wouldn't. Tom pushed the rag harder into my leg as we waited. With my vast medical knowledge of boo-boos, I quickly surmised that I needed a Band-Aid. I stood and bent over, holding the rag in place as I made my way to the house and down the mudroom stairs. I took short, quick steps through the family room, careful not to drip oil or bleed onto the pink shag carpeting, and climbed to the middle of the stairs that led to the kitchen. My teenage sister was sitting at the table, eating. "Donna needs a Band-Aid," Tom said, standing beside me.

"What for?"

"She scratched herself in the barn." I felt the blood soaking through the rag and pressed harder before I bled on the blue stairs.

"Let me see it," Josie said.

"I don't want to come upstairs," I said. "Just throw a Band-Aid down to me."

Josie got up and saw the rag I was holding to my oil-streaked leg. She took me into the mudroom and cleaned me up, using a clean rag to stop the blood. "By the time you grow up that scar will be two inches long," she said. It's not, by the way. When my mother got home from the market she was told by the doctor that it was too late to put stitches in my leg because it had stopped bleeding.

Later that night she said, "I told you you've got no business playing out in that barn. Guess you learned the hard way." Parents always fall back on that.

After I fell out of the apple tree (the same one my mother told me not to climb) and broke my arm, my mom said, "Guess you learned the hard way." After I fell down the stairs (the ones my mother told me not to run on) and broke my other arm, my mom said, "Guess you learned the hard way." And after I broke my first arm *again* trying to jump over a lamp on the end table in the family room while watching *The Carol Burnett Show* (the lamp my mother told me to stop *trying* to jump over), my mom said, "Guess you learned the hard way." I never got to finish that episode of *The Carol Burnett Show.*

My days were filled with as much playtime as I could pack into them. There were plenty of trips to the emergency room but I had fun getting there. That was still the time when mothers told their children to go outside and play, and called them inside at dark to take a bath. If there were problems in the world, I was unaware of them, but that would change.

WHEN I WAS FIVE OR so Tom ran into his garage and I followed. I hated the Taylors' garage. It had a dirt floor that had turned black from what I imagine was junk-car oil leaks and, of course, it smelled. There was always that pervading smell anywhere in the Taylors' house. Kevin was working on his dirt bike. Tom knew all the right buttons to push with his brother and in a flash Kevin was on top of him, smacking him in the head. The whole beating-each-other-up thing was foreign to me. I'd never seen siblings all-out slug each other but the Taylors did it on a daily basis. Tom squirmed and screamed until Kevin released him. "Get out of here, you little shit," he said, kicking Tom's leg. Tom laughed and we turned to go. "Hey," Kevin shouted. "Come here." Tom stepped to him and Kevin pushed him away. "Show me your crotch," he said, looking at me. I had no idea what he meant.

"What's that?" Tom asked.

"Your vagina, you idiot," Kevin said, as he continued to look at me. I still didn't know what he was talking about. He lunged for me and pulled down my shorts. He held them at my ankles and I fell, yanking up my underwear. He laughed at me and I scrambled to my feet, running after Tom again.

In my mind I assumed that Kevin was just being a jerk. He was always a bully and a tormenter to Tom, and I thought that was what he was doing to me. I didn't tell Tess what he did. I didn't even tell Cindy, and when I got home I didn't tell my mother because she might not understand that Kevin was just being an idiot and because of him she might not let me play with Tom anymore. It made perfect sense to me at the time. We always replay scenes in our minds of what we should have done and in those instances we always say and do the right thing. It never happens that way in real life.

TOM PICKED ALL THE BEST places to hide. His house was full of tiny doors that led to a small attic or crawl space but I never went into them. They were dark and smelly, and in my mind I always imagined there'd be rats or snakes in those tight, damp spots. Tom would creep inside one of those small doors and wait for me. He would wait for what felt like hours as I traipsed from room to room looking for him.

I was five or six years old and hadn't entered kindergarten yet when we played hide-and-seek one stifling day. I don't know why we chose to play inside on such a warm day but I heard Tom running through the hallway above me as I counted. Then I heard Kevin yelling, "Get out of here, piss head!" The door closed and I heard Tom scramble farther down the hall. I tiptoed upstairs and pulled open the small attic door at the top of the landing. The attic spaces in the house had long lost any sort of insulation and a blast of heat hit me in the face. Slivers of light streamed into the space and I shut the door. Tom wasn't in there. I looked behind the door of the girls' room and crept to their closet, swinging open the door. Kevin and Tom's door was open and as I walked past I noticed the room was empty. I went into the bathroom at the end of the hall and snatched back the shower curtain. Tom wasn't in the room at the end of the hall, either, so I knew he had to be in his and Kevin's room or that creepy little attic entrance inside the room.

I crept into the room and waded through the clothes and debris on the floor toward the attic door. I reached for the handle when I heard the bedroom door close and lock behind me. I turned to see Kevin; his pants were open. In an instant he grabbed my arms and pushed me to the floor, holding me down. He laughed at me and pulled my face toward his naked body. He laughed louder and I tried to get up to run home but he held me down, pushing my head hard onto the floor. I lost all feeling. No one burst through the door to save me. The walls didn't crumble on, the floor didn't swallow up, and a bolt of lightning didn't strike down what was happening.

I never discovered where Tom was hiding that day. I

think he was probably crouched down inside that attic and stayed there long after I left. I don't know how long I was in that room or remember any details of how I got out the door. I have no memory of walking home or what I did once I got there but I do remember knowing that what had happened was wrong and that I should never talk about it. So I didn't.

Ever.

—◆◆◆—

T W O

We mortals astonish him as much as he us.

—HERMAN MELVILLE, AUTHOR, SPEAKING OF GOD
IN A LETTER TO NATHANIEL HAWTHORNE

I SUPPOSE LOTS OF PROBLEMS with God started when a father "stepped out" for a pack of cigarettes and never came back, when a mother died way too young, when a child was born severely impaired, when a business failed, when an addiction destroyed, or when the cancer spread. I attended the funeral of a five-year-old this week who was accidentally killed. I can't even imagine the problem with God in the middle of that anguish. My problem with God started in Kevin Taylor's bedroom. I was alone and scared, and God didn't do a thing.

I grew up in church. My parents took my sister, my brother, and me every week to church in Brunswick, several miles from Medina. The sign out front said, "The church in the heart of Brunswick with Brunswick on its heart." I looked forward to Sunday school because I loved listening to the stories, especially if it had a flannel graph to go with it. The teacher would put up a figure of Joseph on the flannel graph and then when she got to the part about his coat of many colors that his dad gave to him she'd put a tiny robe with green, purple, yellow, and blue stripes on top of the figure. On and on the story would go until the flannel graph was covered. Each week after the service, Preacher Bill would bend down and I'd kiss his cheek. He did that every week until he died of a heart attack on the day his oldest son, Richard, was being ordained at his graduation from seminary. I was still a little girl. He was a good man and he left behind his widow to figure out a new way to live. Richard, fresh out of seminary, became our new pastor and more than thirty years and several grandchildren later is still pastoring at "The church in the heart of Brunswick with Brunswick on its heart."

At some point during those early church years I became aware of a verse in the book of Galatians that says, "God had special plans for me and set me apart for his work even before I was born. He called me through his grace." I did believe God loved me. The flannel-graph stories emphasized his love every week. I believed he created me (the Psalmist said God created and knit us together in our mother's womb. In the book of Isaiah God says, "It is I who made the earth and created mankind upon it"); I just couldn't believe he had *special* plans for *me*. Special plans were for special girls. What happened inside Kevin Taylor's bedroom didn't happen to special girls, just girls like me. I think that became my problem with God, too.

No one taught me to keep things hidden but shame is a great motivator for secrecy. It's a natural response, like breathing in and out. I believed that what happened was my fault. If I hadn't gone into Kevin's bedroom to look for Tom none of it would have happened. I was in a room that was off limits (I had no business being in there) and made Kevin angry. I was responsible for his actions. I had a hard time trusting anyone after that. Years later my father's friend Raymond visited one afternoon and he knelt down for a hug. My mother said, "Well, go ahead, give Raymond a hug," but I just stood there. I couldn't do it. I distrusted a hug, an arm around the shoulder, or a simple pat on the back. If I couldn't trust people I sure couldn't trust God.

I don't remember playing with Tom after that day of hide-and-seek. I don't recall ever crossing through the field again to get to his house or his playing at my home but I imagine we continued to go on as if nothing ever happened. I don't remember when the Taylors moved or if I said good-bye. My memories of them ended on that day. Author Maya Angelou was asked at a symposium what she considered to be the most profound evil in society and she said sexual abuse against a child because one sexual act takes that child from the innocence of knowing nothing, to the cynicism of believing nothing. I was a cynic before I entered kindergarten.

I WAS SPIT ON IN second grade. My class was walking single file to the library when we passed a class of sixth graders. It was there, in that brief passing, that someone hocked a loogie. I never saw it coming. The "hock-er" didn't aim it *at* me but I was the one to wear it. I felt something wet on my hand but when I looked nothing was there. It was only when our class approached the library door that I realized something was oozing down my maroon polyester-blend turtleneck. This wasn't a backwoods school in the middle of nowhere; it was the Ella Canavan Elementary School, and even today this single spitting incident is probably the only one to have blackened the history of the school. I didn't want to draw attention to what happened so I walked in silence into the library and then crept up to Mrs. Brewer's side. She was talking with the librarian so I waited, never glancing down at what was oozing toward the bottom of my shirt.

"Go find your seat," Mrs. Brewer said. Mrs. Brewer was only in her fifties when I entered her classroom in 1974, but from my perspective I thought she was at least a hundred and two. She was short and solid but could get our attention with a sharp, quick snap of her fingers. I wondered if I should bother her with this. "Do you need to go to the bathroom?" she asked. She stared at me. I hated to be a nuisance but this was too much.

"Somebody hockered on me," I whispered, using a word I'd heard my brother use dozens of times.

"Somebody what?" Mrs. Brewer said.

I pointed to my shirt. "Hockered on me."

Mrs. Brewer leaped for the tissues on the librarian's desk. "Oh for the love of . . . who did this?" she asked, scooping the glob from my shirt. I shrugged. "Savages," she whispered, wiping the remains with a new tissue and leaving a stain of white particles clinging where the snot had been. "They blindsided you." I wasn't familiar with that word. "You didn't see it coming," she said. She reached inside her dress pocket and pulled out a small sucker for me, winking. "That's how it goes sometimes."

As we plan our lives we never say, "First, I'm going to start off my dream with hardship. Then somewhere along the way I want to sprinkle a year or two of clinical depression onto it, some sexual abuse, an addiction would be nice, maybe a stint at rehab, an accident would be exciting, a divorce or two would be thrilling, and then I want to top the dream off with agony. Agony would be great!" We don't do that. We tie our dreams up with ribbons, bows, balloons, and streamers, and aim for the mountaintop but get life in the valley instead. And at some point it's there, wandering in the valley, when we realize that life doesn't turn out the way we planned. We get blindsided with something far greater than a giant loogie. Questions never get answered, confusion sets in, and once we clean ourselves up the best we know how we realize we're still left with the stain of it all. Like Mrs. Brewer said, that's how it goes sometimes. True. But it seems we're rarely told that the dream doesn't die there. I just assumed it did.

MY MOTHER HOPED THAT THE farmhouse would be torn down after the Taylors moved but before long we heard that new tenants would be renting it. When the Taylors moved they left a huge pile of stuff inside the garage. My brother, Brian, and I decided to forage through that mess one day in hopes of finding an odd treasure or two. We had just begun to wade through the massive garbage heap when a car pulled into the driveway. A fat man opened the driver's side door and pointed his chubby finger at us.

"What are you kids doing here?" We mumbled something about going through the Taylors' stuff they left behind. "This is *my* house and *my* junk pile," he said. "Now get out of here." It was a promising beginning.

Larry Swann was overweight and smoked too much and his wife, LeAnne, like Tess before her, never worked and always, I mean *always*, wore a bathrobe. I think she had several but they were all pale cotton, snapped in the front and fell to just below the knee. The Swanns had two teenage sons, Martin and Randy, who smelled like b.o. and cigarettes. Larry had a series of jobs over the years, one of the most interesting being lead singer of a family Southern gospel band. During many rehearsals in their garage we could feel the throbbing of the bass through our kitchen window (keep in mind the noise had to *cross* a field to get to us). At some point Larry realized there was little money to be made for a no-name Southern gospel act with the background singer sporting a bathrobe so he tried his hand at being a preacher. I don't remember what denomination, but does it really matter?

My mother stood in the backyard one day and watched as a couple of men began digging in the back of the Swanns' property, near our garden. "What are they doing?" I asked.

"Lord only knows," she said, sighing.

Days later we discovered they were digging a baptismal. If you're a self-proclaimed preacher then you *must* have a watering hole in which to baptize the flock. Of course, neither Preacher Larry nor any of the men out there knew how to dig a pond or about proper drainage but that didn't matter. Soon, the massive hole was dug and ready for rain. It took a while and the cavity eventually filled with water but by that time the mosquitoes had discovered the muddy chasm and set up small cities and malls. As we worked in the garden we could hear the deep guttural throb of the frogs that called the baptismal home. My mother would sigh and shake her head and eventually got to the point where she never even looked at the hole brimming with brown, foamy scum.

Randy and my brother, Brian, would do things together and from time to time. Randy would come to our house, filling the kitchen with the subtle aroma of sweat and

Marlboros. He would have smelled better after a quick dip in the baptismal. I was in sixth grade and my friend Peggy Long was over playing one afternoon when Randy walked into the yard. Peg and I could play for hours together. We loved to put on little shows with our Barbie dolls, sometimes constructing a house for them out of a shoebox. The only problem was that Barbie's much taller than a shoebox unless you turn it on end but then the house is too skinny. We tried to use a dog cage at Peg's house one day but it smelled so bad neither one of us could hold Barbie inside for very long without gagging.

Peggy and I were running through the yard when Randy joined us. I hadn't even seen him cross the field.

"I'll play freeze tag if you want," he said.

"Nah," I said. I didn't want to play with him.

"You just know I'll beat you," Randy said, running after me. I scrambled away and he tagged Peg, freezing her in place. I zoomed around the red maple and smacked Peggy's hand, unfreezing her. Randy plowed into me from behind and I fell to the ground. He fell on top of me laughing and I could smell his b.o. I felt suffocated and tried to squeeze out from beneath him. He held me down, humping my back.

There would be no replaying of the scene in my mind

later of what I should have done. There comes a time when everything within you rises up and shouts, Never again! I will never again let someone abuse me. I will never again let someone intimidate me. I will never again let someone manipulate me. This was my time. I felt anger, loathing, and revulsion rise in my chest. Randy's hands were squarely on the ground by my face. The vein that ran between his thumb and index finger bulged under his weight. In a swift second I turned my head and clamped my teeth down on his right hand. He screamed, jumping off of me and shaking his hand in the air.

"Leave me alone, you bastard!" I had never used language like that; I don't even know where I'd heard it—my parents didn't curse!

Peg's eyes bulged. "Good grief," she said. "What are you doing?" She had missed what happened so I didn't talk about it, packing the incident away.

I should have run and told my mother or any other safe adult around me first about Kevin and then about Randy but I didn't. On any given Sunday, when Preacher Powers knelt down for my kiss I could have whispered in his ear that I needed to tell him something and I know he would have listened. But I passed off the Randy occasion as something that wasn't that bad, no big deal. It was just a one-time thing: we were playing tag, my clothes were still on, and I hadn't ended up in the hospital so really there was no harm done. Just like the molestation in Kevin's bedroom years earlier I maintained the belief that so much of what happened was my fault. *I shouldn't have been playing in the front yard. When he said he wanted to play, I should have just walked into the house.* I wasn't "molested" this time so I denied the confusion and just sucked it up because it worked for me.

IN J. R. R. TOLKIEN'S *The Hobbit,* the great magician Gandolf tells Bilbo Baggins, "There is more to you than you know." Bilbo had more than just Baggins blood running through his veins, he had blood from the mighty Took clan. The author of Ecclesiastes says God has set eternity in our hearts. Our lineage is both human and divine, making us not the presumed earthlings on a spiritual jaunt but rather spiritual beings on a human journey.

The whole body/soul relationship can be awkward and strained. Our bodies are made for earthly use while our souls have been outfitted for a heavenly one. Leonardo DaVinci said, "You think that the body is a wonderful work. In reality this is nothing compared to the soul that inhabits in that structure . . . It is the work of God." We can see and care for our bodies, but our soul is of another realm altogether. It's other-worldly. If we want to know what's inside our souls we must get to know God and discern what he placed there and just like Bilbo, we'll discover that there's more to us than we know. If our soul is never nourished, if it is kept tucked away from its eternal purpose then it will seek nourishment somewhere else as we pour ourselves into things like career, learning, organizations, governing bodies, drugs, or sex, in an effort to fill the heavenly sized gap. Like all of us, I was born with an eternal perspective but somewhere along this human path I lost it. If my problem with God was that I thought he should have done more on that sweltering day in Kevin's bedroom, then his problem with me was that I gave up on him. Not outwardly; I think it was more of a pleasant indifference.

My deception lay in the fact that I presumed I was the one to pull it all together, leaving little room for Providence. Augustine said God gives where he finds empty hands. My hands were full of plans and dreams that *I* had determined to make happen. I had no need for God or his help so I had no need for grace. I was still too young to comprehend that someday my strength would be inadequate and if I wasn't careful I'd miss the great understanding of that.

PEGGY'S DAD DIED WHEN SHE was twelve. His liver just couldn't tolerate one more drink. On her second day of absence I called and asked where she had been.

"My dad died," she said.

I'd never known anyone my age whose parent had died. It couldn't be possible. "He did not," I said.

"He did. He died last night."

"You're kidding?" I chalk that question up to being young and stupid. As if she was going to say, *Yes, I am. Isn't that hysterical?*

Peg and I were in the same math class and I was so grateful because she was great in math and I struggled through every second of the hour. My blood ran cold thinking about problems like: *If Train A leaves Birmingham carrying a load of coal and Train B leaves Birmingham carrying a load of chickens, which train will make it to Boston in time for dinner?*

Our seats were located in front of four of the princesses of the school. They were every teacher's delight, so beautiful, charming, and trendy, wearing their Izod alligator polo shirts and crisp khaki pants. Peggy and I wore Toughskin corduroys (their slogan was, "The toughest of Sears tough jeans . . . lab tests prove it!"), sported either a bad perm or an uneven haircut, and never made anybody's cool list. I had eight teeth pulled ("Her mouth is just way too small for all those teeth," the orthodontist told my mother) and got braces. I was forced to wear a headgear for eight hours a day. Many classmates had the cool headgear that simply wrapped around the back of the neck and attached to the braces. One of the princesses modeled this fashionable headgear. My headgear looked like a brain-sucking device used in a mad scientist's lab from an old 1930s horror movie. It sat on my head like a helmet and attacked my teeth from all sides. I put it on as soon as I got off the bus and never wore it in front of small children or anyone with a pacemaker.

Our math teacher was a man with a red face. It wasn't sunburn or even a healthy glow; it was just red . . . all the time. Mr. Teacher Man (I'll call him Mr. TM from now on) seemed to be on the backside of his teaching career. Not because he was old but because he seemed to hate the job, or maybe he just disliked Peg and me. I don't know.

He asked Peggy and me to go to the chalkboard one day and I could feel my stomach turn. For someone who is admittedly horrible in math, why put me through the public humiliation? We walked to the board and I knocked the

◆ 3 0 ◆

eraser to the floor. Peg and I both bent for it and klunked our heads together like two of the Three Stooges. The class laughed but Mr. TM did not. We were wasting his time.

Mr. TM always wanted us to keep a piece of scratch paper to do our math problems on during quizzes. A few weeks after Peg's dad died we were given a pop quiz. (Those two words can still strike horror in me.) Since Peggy was a math whiz her paper was usually clean with the exception of a problem or two. Mine looked as if I was trying to disprove Einstein's theory of relativity. After Peggy finished the quiz she gathered her papers to turn them in and said beneath her breath, "I don't have any scratch paper."

Being the dummy that I was I whispered, "What?"

She said, "I don't have any scratch paper."

Now at this time, our verbalizing during a quiz had caught the attention of Mr. TM and he stormed to our desks. His red face had turned a deep shade of purple. Purple! I cowered at the sight but Peggy remained strong. "What did you say?" he bellowed down to her.

"I said, 'I didn't have any scratch paper,'" she said.

"What did you say?" he bellowed again.

His face was turning a deeper shade of purple. He was

like an eggplant with eyes. I just sat and trembled. My grade was already poor enough. I didn't need these quiz results thrown out.

"I said, 'I don't have any scratch paper,'" Peg said, now for the fourth time for those who were counting and I'm sure they were . . . it *was* math class.

"What did *you* say?" Mr. TM boomed, looking at me.

I broke out in a sweat and could hear my heart in my ears. My hands shook and a pain raced through my arm. I was having a heart attack in math class! I could feel the princesses staring at the back of my head. "I said, 'What,'" I managed to squeak.

"Do *you* have scratch paper?" he asked.

"Lots," I said, holding up my reams. For a brief moment I was so proud of my ineptitude.

"Are you girls cheating?" he said, his face turning a softer shade of purple now.

I wanted to say, "Look at my grades. I'm just hoping to balance a checkbook someday." Peg and I both shook our heads.

"Don't ever talk in my class again," he said, snatching the papers from us.

In the weeks following the scratch-paper incident a school assembly was called. A special speaker was coming to entertain the student body. We'd never heard of the person before but it didn't matter; he was going to entertain us. Peg and I threw our books in our lockers and made our way to the gymnasium. There were prime seats down front. We wouldn't have chosen those seats if it was just the principal addressing us but this was an entertainer! We trudged down the bleachers and ran onto the gym floor, crossing over to the other side for the good seats. We had climbed up two bleachers for our perfect spot when we heard him.

"Those aren't available." We turned to see Mr. TM, whose eyes were scanning the gym floor. I didn't think he was talking to us and moved toward the seats again. "Those seats are taken, girls."

Peg and I looked at him but his eyes were still on the gym floor. By that time every good bleacher was filled and we trekked up to the top row. I sat down and was positioning myself behind Ralphie the teenage giant boy when I noticed the four princesses cross the gym floor for "our" seats down below.

It turns out that Mr. TM was right. The best seats were unavailable . . . to us. Those seats were special and for special girls. We could make do somewhere else. In my mind I always assumed that Mr. TM didn't like Peg and me. It never dawned on me that maybe he didn't like himself or his job or his circumstances, whatever they were, and it never occurred to me that although he was a teacher that he was still a jerk. His saving seats at a school assembly like a lovesick teenager was not our problem, it was his. The fact that he never offered an ounce of compassion to Peggy after the death of her father but instead bellowed in her face over scratch paper was not her problem but *his*.

Funny how people color the way we feel about ourselves. Somewhere along the way sociologists termed that as the looking-glass self: We begin to perceive ourselves as those around us see us. *You're a good student but not as good as your sister. You're a great athlete but not nearly as strong as your brother. You're a good dancer but she's amazing. You're thin but just not thin enough for the job. You're too fat for the job. You're a good mom but have you seen her remarkable home and kids? You're a good man but not nearly half the man as my father! The best seats are available but not for you!* Countless books, magazine articles, and television shows are dedicated to helping us be better in every way so we can finally reach those coveted best seats.

François Rabelais, the French Renaissance writer and physician asked, "When you say the word *God*, what does it mean to you?" Sitting atop the bleachers behind Ralphie the teenage giant boy I don't think I really knew what I thought about God. It was years later I realized that what I thought of myself would come only when I believed, not just thought it to be true, but really *believed* that I was chosen, accepted, and loved by God, not for anything that I could do for him but simply because that's what he does. He loves. It didn't matter what Mr. TM or the princesses thought or even what I thought of myself. God had created the best seats in the entire assembly for me. I just didn't know that yet.

THREE

... the voice we should listen to most as we choose a vocation is the voice that we might think we should listen to least, and that is the voice of our own gladness. What can we do that makes us the gladdest ... ? Is it making things with our hands out of wood, or stone or paper or canvas? Or is it making something we hope like truth out of words? Or is it making people laugh or weep in a way that cleanses their spirit? I believe that if it is a thing that makes us truly glad, then it is a good thing and it is our thing and it is the calling voice that we were made to answer with our lives.

—FREDERICK BUECHNER, AUTHOR
Secrets in the Dark: A Life in Sermons
(New York: HarperOne, 2006)

PEGGY AND I WENT OUR separate ways after eighth grade. One of the last laughs we shared was on the last day of school when in an ironic move Mr. TM, who was caught up in the euphoria of the final day, bumped into Peg in the hall and hugged her, flattening the origami craft she was holding. "He smashed my origami," she said, trying to puff out the bird's crushed chest. "Of *all* the people to give me a hug," she said. "Look at my origami!" I laughed till I cried. We had been the best of friends, but things changed after that summer. I loved acting and choir and shows in high school, and Peggy loved boys. I wasn't ready for boys because I'd had enough of them already. Peg and I lost our common ground but we managed to smile at each other in the halls in that awkward, I-think-I-have-the-stomach-virus kind of way.

I acted my way through high school. I was one of the introverts who couldn't talk in front of five people but was at ease on the school stage. When people watched me on stage I never felt like they were watching me but rather the character I was playing, and I threw myself into roles like Miss Hannigan from *Annie*, an ugly stepsister in *Cinderella*, and Aunt Abby in *Arsenic and Old Lace*. I anticipated every school production but those wretched math and science classes became more difficult in high school. At one point I had a math tutor who was a senior. She was a cheerleader and her father was one of the coaches for the Cleveland Browns. She was perky and pretty but it's hard to stay focused on teaching math when you're perky and pretty because the boys just can't deny such perkiness attention during tutoring sessions. I gave up the tutor and trudged along, even making the honor roll several times (when a math or science class wasn't on my schedule) and loved high school.

Just like in elementary school my favorite classes were ones that had anything to do with words or stories. I loved history because that was one lonnng story. I loved my accelerated reading class because I got to read lots of things really fast, and I loved English and literature. During my junior year I was sitting in Mrs. Lenk's literature class when Mrs. Elrick, the advanced placement English teacher, knocked on the door. She was blond and brilliant, and taught in the corner classroom at the end of the hall. All the top-dog seniors were in her class. I'd pass her door on the corner and see all the top dogs lapping up her knowledge of the English language as I scurried off to math, my scratch paper dangling from every book I owned. After the two teachers conversed, Mrs. Lenk came beside me and whispered that Mrs. Elrick wanted to speak to me in the hallway. What had I done? Had I inadvertently cut off one of her top dogs in the lunch line? What gross misjustice had I inflicted?

"How are you?" Mrs. Elrick said, folding her arms around her sweater.

"Fine."

She got right down to business. "I'd like you to be in my A.P. class next year." I was silent. Shock does that to you. "Your grades are excellent in literature but interaction is crucial to the A.P. class. Each student must participate and that worries me about you." I stood speechless. "You walk through these halls and sit in classes like a little mouse but then you get on stage and the teachers say, 'Who is that?' You're a different person up there. You can clearly hear the language of words but I'm wondering if you can be that person you are on stage in my class. Can you verbally participate?" I nodded my head, which wasn't a good sign.

I made it into Mrs. Elrick's A.P. class and said one word all year. One morning she asked me to name the predominant imagery used in *Native Son*. I hated answering questions in class. I preferred to listen and take notes. So often another student would talk and talk and talk, and I'd think, *Less is more, you know.* Or one student would say something and two minutes later another student would say the same thing only with different adjectives and verbs. As a bonafide introvert it was not unusual for someone else to

verbalize my thoughts before I mustered up enough chutz-
pah to speak up but I'd always nod with great enthusiasm
like, *Oh yes! I agree. Tremendous thought.*

Mrs. Elrick leaned on her desk and looked at me.
"What was the predominant imagery in *Native Son?*"

I looked at the girl across the room. She was the one
who always sucked the thoughts right out of my head and
said them before me. Why wasn't she answering now? I
felt my heart beat faster. "Light," I said, wiping my palms
on my jeans.

Mrs. Elrick smiled. "Very good, *Donna.*" She emphasized my name because in her heart she knew it'd be the
only time I'd ever participate in the class she had *invited* me
to join.

Mrs. Elrick said I could hear the language of words. I
didn't recognize it but my life was telling me something. I
couldn't hear the language of numbers like Peggy or of
music like my friends in band, but I could hear and feel
the language of words. Eternity speaks to our soul in the
language that is meant just for us, the language *we* can understand. When I flip through snapshots in my mind of
my early life they include reading stories to my mother
each evening in bed, being the first in line for library time,
listening intently to the flannel-graph lesson in Sunday

school, making up stories with Peggy, relaxing as I entered a history, English, or literature classroom, and feeling at home on stage. All of these situations were spoken to me in a language that I could understand.

In one form or another we are all going to answer with our lives to something and that choice either leads to freedom or stagnation. Although I was only in high school I'd seen more than enough people who never honored the raw material they'd been given and who lived in a state of chronic resignation, just sticking it out to the end. I was at the time of my life when it was clear to other people that I could hear the language of words but I was still unaware of that calling voice.

I WENT TO CHURCH WITH an African American girl named Ebbie Radcliff. She and her family were the only black people in the entire church. During the early years, back when Preacher Bill was our pastor, another black man named Clarence and his wife came for quite some time. He wore a yellow suit. No one else in our church owned a yellow suit, not even the women. After some time he took his yellow suit and went somewhere else leaving the Radcliffs to stick it out alone in a sea of white faces. Bill Radcliff was a deacon and Sunday schoolteacher, and his wife, Oma, also taught Sunday school. No one in church could smile like Mr. and Mrs. Radcliff. Some people looked bored, even aggravated to be at church on Sunday, but Bill and Oma lit up the place. They both died too young. Bill and Oma had three children, all girls, and I played with Ebbie, the youngest. When Ebbie went off to college she chose Cedarville University, three hours south of where we lived. I'd never heard of Cedarville but Ebbie let me look through her yearbooks and I thought it looked swell. Yes, *swell.*

And that's how I chose my institution of higher learning. I never even visited the campus! I don't recommend that method to anyone choosing a new sofa, let alone a college but that's how I did it. Cedarville sent me a package of information and they had a traveling speech and drama team, and put on several stage productions a year so I thought, Why not?

I worked several summer jobs after high school in preparation for college. I cleaned hotel rooms in the morning (I once refused to clean a room filled with sex toys and video cameras, the manager took one look inside, rolled his eyes, and closed the door behind him) and worked as a waitress in a pizza joint in the afternoon. "The tips alone will buy all your textbooks in college," the owner said. "And you'll have more hours than you want to work." I was soon demoted to dishwasher when his favorite waitress decided to come work for him again. "I don't need two waitresses for this shift," he said without looking at me. "If you still want to work during this time of day then you'll need to wash dishes. The shift ends two hours earlier because we don't get enough customers to keep a dishwasher on all that time." What a jerk. Heat rose to my head as he talked. His "favorite" waitress had quit weeks ago and I'd been on the job two weeks when she decided she liked the tips after all. Shouldn't he have hired *her* to wash the dishes since he already had a new waitress? "So what d'ya say?" he asked, looking at me. *I say you're a jerk,* I thought, but I knew if I wanted to keep my hours cleaning hotel rooms in the morning then I'd need the dishwashing job in the afternoon. When Burger King opened I applied for the night shift and ended up working with Peggy. Four years of lost friendship was recaptured during the first night of work together. We scrubbed urinals and mopped the kitchen while tall, blond Mindy wiped anything gummy from the individual ketchup packets. It felt like Mr. TM's class all over again. *You two go clean the urinals because the good seats here by the ketchup packets are taken.*

* * *

DURING MY FRESHMAN YEAR OF college I realized that if I wanted to be a working actress, I would really need to move to New York or Los Angeles, and those weren't the best options for a bookworm who wanted to get married and have children, so I added broadcasting as another major. Already my ideal dream of being an actress was changing but broadcasters use words, right?

I dated a guy that year who was gregarious and funny. From now on I'll just refer to him as "The Boyfriend." The Boyfriend could make me laugh and I've always liked being around people who can make me laugh. I had a friend that year named Ladd who was a brilliant geek. Everyone knew he'd run a Fortune 500 company some day. One afternoon at lunch several friends and I were sitting around talking and laughing when Ladd said he didn't want to have children because he didn't want to populate hell with his offspring. A pall fell over the lunch table. Ladd *wasn't* funny. I didn't hang out with him much. On the other hand, The Boyfriend could keep lunch banter hopping along with amusing and ridiculous stories. He had a carefree, easy way about him and was fun to be with but his parents hated me. His mother said that because of the major I had chosen I would never make a good wife and would end up leaving him. The Boyfriend never said they were being judgmental or absurd or idiots. He just smiled in his carefree, easy way and let them go on despising my major and me.

The Boyfriend's parents would never come see a play I was in or acknowledge awards I won in Forensics, the traveling speech and drama team. "Good grief, son! She's *already* out running around with actors. Can't you see the writing on the wall?" Unlike Mrs. Elrick, they never acknowledged that I could hear the language of words because to them words were going to be my downfall. The Boyfriend's parents belonged to the club of the superspiritual. They listened to boring music, awakened extra early for spiritual reading, refused to go to movies, and did not allow books into their home that didn't have a Godly bent. No one, not even God himself, could live up to their expectations.

"What sort of faith do you have?" The Boyfriend's mother asked me one day during a visit to their home. She was ironing The Boyfriend's father's shirt and her brow looked pained. If a pinched nerve could have a face it would have been hers. She was misery holding an iron.

"Faith in God," I said, looking around for an exit.

"How much faith do you have?" She didn't look at me as she sprayed starch onto the collar. It had to be stiff. Really, really stiff.

A shiver of fright ran down my spine and I searched my purse for my plane ticket home. "Uh . . . well, not enough I'm sure," I said, my compact slipping through my sweaty fingers.

She flipped the shirt and attacked the collar with small, firm strokes. "You should work at getting more faith."

"How do you work at getting more faith?" I asked, dumping the contents of my purse onto the table. Lipstick, wallet, speech notes about fungus, but no plane ticket!

"You just *work* at it," she said.

I uttered something that sounded like the bleating of a sheep and fled the room. For months afterward that conversation played through my head. *How much faith do you have?* The Boyfriend's mother asked. I wish I had responded, "How much is *enough?*" Don't we need just enough to help us take that first step toward God? Time after time in the pages of the Bible he simply says, "Come." Don't wash up, no need to take off your shoes, just come. Take a step. Isn't faith a trip through the day without a map? And doesn't a genuine faith naturally spring from getting to know God better and doesn't that happen with each step? The Boyfriend's parents didn't realize that it's our human plight to be imperfect and that it's right *there* in that imperfection that we receive grace, and *that's* how we come to know God better. Like all the superspiritual, The Boyfriend's parents were so supersized in their spirituality that they had no need for grace. They had forgotten that it was the lop-sided souls, the prostitutes, the divorcees, and the terminal who followed Christ while he was on earth. It was never the religious scholars. They had so much head knowledge that they didn't need the gift of grace walking amongst them in Palestine. The superspiritual, like the superintellectual, are rigid and unapproachable. Through the life of Christ I see that honest, true, and pure spirituality is completely accessible and grace-filled.

In college I had read that Thomas Aquinas said the splendor of a soul in grace is so seductive that it surpasses the beauty of all created things. In The Boyfriend's parents I discovered there is *nothing* seductive about a person who speaks the harsh language of ungrace, but sometimes, when it is spoken to us, we must recognize it as a *gift* of grace. God was showing me all the reasons to get out of my relationship with The Boyfriend. One afternoon Ladd caught up to me on the sidewalk leading to my dorm and we talked about his upcoming graduation. "You'll get any job you want," I said. "You have everything it takes."

Ladd shook his head. "No, I don't. I can't talk to people like you can. I'll never be able to communicate and use words the way you do. I wish I could but I'm just not gifted that way." Ladd wasn't funny; as a matter of fact he was as unfunny as anyone I've ever known. He was all business and brains but he saw the way I used words as a gift. I'd never thought about it that way and his comment stayed with me for weeks. The Boyfriend eventually stopped smiling and laughing, and took to heart what his parents believed about me: Words were not a gift and any life with me would be doomed.

Every moment we walk this earth I believe our soul is guiding us toward something greater, something beyond ourselves, while our reasoning pulls us back into something less, building upon the sands of what Leo Tolstoy called the unstable house of our brief, illusive life. The conflict always remains but the choice is ours. The Boyfriend and I broke up. When I look over my life, that event became my first comprehension of grace.

ON MY FIRST DAY OF college the broadcasting students had all been invited to a mixer. I'd never been to a mixer

before and it sounded so collegy. A handful of students fil-
tered into the room and a guy named Troy VanLiere
talked to me. He was warm and down to earth and had the
cutest, most genuine smile I'd ever seen. "I'm from upstate
New York," he said.

"Why do you call it upstate?" I asked.

"Because it's upstate."

"Like in the northern section of the state?"

"Right."

"Then why don't you just call it northern New York?"

"Why would we do that when we call it upstate?"

I didn't have a good answer. Troy had auburn hair and
eyes that were green or sometimes gray, depending on
what he was wearing, and he was funny. I told Bob Gresh,
one of our college friends, that Troy was the funniest person I knew. Bob said I lived a sad, sheltered life.

Troy and I were friends for two and a half years then
started dating at the end of our junior year (The Boyfriend
had graduated and married the perfect girl with ideal
faith). Troy's parents never questioned my major (it *was*
the same as their son's after all) or my faith, and they actually seemed to like me. At the beginning of our senior
year I told Troy that someday I was going to write a book

and the first line would be: *It was raining real hard the day we buried my daddy.* I had no idea what the book would be about but I loved the sound of that line in my head. I never told The Boyfriend about my book idea. I never trusted him enough to share something as far-fetched as the idea of writing a book. I just knew he'd tell his parents and after they made me feel stupid the very notion would institutionalize them. "She wants to write a book?! Son, how can she write a book *and* tend to you and your children? Everything's going black. Where are the smelling salts?" I felt safe with Troy.

I asked Troy to come to my and my roommate's apartment to study one night. Before he got there I was struck with a virus that hurled me to the bathroom (pun intended). Troy waited in the living room and when I exited the bathroom I lay on the sofa. After a while I said, "I'm sorry I made you come over. You can head home if you want."

"That's okay," he said. "I don't mind if you're sick or quiet or whatever. I just like being in the space you're in." I knew he was a good soul. The Boyfriend would have left on winged feet.

Troy asked me to marry him later that year. I thought,

"Didn't you get that memo, God? That dark haired, blue-eyed memo I sent up back when I was five?" When I considered Troy's goodness toward me it was as if God said, "Yeah, I got that memo but I thought I'd give you something better than you think you deserve."

I didn't know it then but *that* is the language of grace.

FOUR

Boy, whatever you is and wherever you is, don't be what
you ain't, because when you is what you ain't, you isn't.

—UNCLE REMUS, FICTIONAL CHARACTER
OF WRITER JOEL CHANDLER HARRIS

TROY HAD TO COMPLETE AN internship so right after
graduation he moved to Nashville to work in a music studio assisting sound engineers. That internship turned into
a job and after we married in November 1989, I joined him
and found work at a small, struggling radio station basi-
cally doing whatever needed to be done. I auditioned for
plays or commercials when I could but there wasn't a lot of
acting jobs in Nashville at that time. "You'd be much better
off going to New York," an acting coach told me. "There's
no work here."

Before we had gotten married Troy and I had talked

about having children. We wanted to work for a few years to save some money and then start our family. On several occasions Troy mentioned that he'd love to have two or three children and then adopt a child or two. I said, "No, no. I've seen those TV reports about how hard it is for people to adopt. They should have first right to children who need to be adopted." What a noble person I was.

A year or so into our marriage I told Troy about Kevin Taylor. Troy had pointed out more than once that I had the tendency to be a lone ranger. While carrying in five bags of grocery: "You know, I could have helped you with those." *No, no. I've got them.* While moving the sofa to the opposite wall in the living room: "I could have helped you do that." *No, no. Just as easy to do it myself.* My silent motto could have been: no help, no hurt. I had become self-reliant to a fault and still kept things close to the vest, never fully trusting anyone.

I told Troy as much as I could about that time in Kevin's bedroom and in the next breath he said, "Why do you sound like it was your fault? It wasn't." It registered as sound in my ears but nothing more.

During this time I met a man from a publishing company who was overseeing the recording of a musical score in the studio where Troy worked. I saw him quite often when I visited and one day he asked if I'd be interested in writing the dialogue for a new musical he needed written. He didn't know that I'd been writing as long as I could remember; he simply said he thought I'd do a great job with the script. It never dawned on me to say no. That job turned into several more in the years to come and opened up doors to write short sketches or a full production here and there for charity fund-raisers.

Soon after the radio station shut down I found a job working in sales for a communications company but still took in writing work on the side. Since I worked full time it was harder to go on auditions, but even when I did find acting work my soul wasn't satisfied with it. I didn't have aspirations to be an extra in music videos, a customer in a car commercial, or a housewife having trouble with my vacuum for an infomercial. Each acting gig, like the sales position, became just a job. A few months into the sales job a man contacted me from a publishing company about writing the dialogue for a full-production musical. I was excited about the possibility but after trading several phone calls with the man I never understood his expectations for the project. One evening Troy asked what the man wanted me to do and I said, "I have no idea. He still hasn't given me any real answers."

Troy said, "Then maybe you aren't asking the right questions."

That was the mantra of my life: get the answers before asking myself the right questions. *What do I really love to do?* The writer of Ecclesiastes said that a man "can do nothing better than to eat and drink and find satisfaction in all his toil—*this is the gift of God.*" A divine present for each of us. A few breaths later the writer says man "seldom reflects on the days of his life, because God keeps him occupied with gladness of heart." I missed that question somewhere along the way: *What makes my heart glad?* The Declaration of Independence says we have the right to the pursuit of happiness, we can chase after it all the days of our life. God promised gladness, not just a pursuit but an occupation of the heart. My problem was I didn't believe any of that.

I knew so many people who tolerated their jobs. I'd ask a friend about his job and he'd sigh a pitiful "okay" with a shrug of the shoulders. I figured we were all in this together, working okay jobs with an okay salary, just hobbling along as best we could on this okay journey. I hated sales but figured the paycheck was decent so I could make do. Every now and then the deep philosophical words of Uncle Remus would ring through my head: *Boy, whatever you is and wherever you is, don't be what you ain't, because when you is what you ain't, you isn't.* Unfortunately, I never asked myself the question, "What ain't you?"

The deepest questions I asked at that time were, *How much does it pay?* Or, *How much time off for vacation?* I never asked my life the deep and abiding questions about purpose, meaning, or value, or what if I gained the whole world and lost my soul. In a magazine article at work I read that Aiden Wilson Tozer said that the most important question we will ever ask ourselves is, "What do I really think about God?" Staring at my cubicle walls I thought he had special plans for some people but not for others. I thought he loved some people more than others. I thought his love was typically based on performance, giving all of us what we deserve.

Weeks later I read that on her deathbed novelist Gertrude Stein's last words were, "What is the answer?" Without a reply she then asked, "In that case . . . what is the question?" I didn't know what that meant but thought perhaps Gertrude was still questioning the meaning of life as she drew her last breath. Maybe questioning was the beginning of hearing. My life was begging me to ask the important questions but I lived without giving an ear to the Divine Whisper in my soul; threatening to become deaf to the loudest shouts of direction. I was continuously disappointed in my work but thought that if I was supposed to make a change, I'd get that signal through thunderclaps and lightning.

The film *Amazing Grace* depicts the life of William Wilberforce, a member of British Parliament who brought bill after bill before parliament for nearly twenty years in his attempts to end the slave trade in England. In one scene Wilberforce turned to his old preacher, John Newton, a former slave-ship owner for guidance. "God sometimes does his work with gentle drizzle, not storms," Newton said.

I never heard thunder peals or saw flashes of lightning but a steady drizzle of writing work continued to pour in from different places. I never noticed. I was writing short- or full-length productions complete with plot and character but couldn't distinguish the plot of my own life and the story that was being revealed. Grace is subtle that way. It never knocks you over the head but caresses your soul. That's the tricky part in discerning it. We want storms and hurricanes to capture our attention but get silent breath; and like breath grace moves in and out, in and out, every moment of every day, always present, and always so easy to miss.

Each time I received a request to write a script for a short sketch or full production I was eager to begin but I began to cringe at technical work. I drove home after work one afternoon and sat down at the computer to begin a job of writing the instructions for a piece of computer software. It sounded like such a simple job. After an hour sitting in front of the computer I was still at ground zero. When Troy got home from work I explained the job to him and he said, "They hired *you* to write the instructions for this software?" I nodded. "And you said YES?" he asked. Troy knew long before I did the kind of writing that suited me. Troy wrote the instructions (he's a closet computer geek) and I received the paycheck. My life was saying, "When you is what you ain't, you isn't," but the paycheck was great and really, isn't that what it's all about? No more broken limbs, but I was still learning the hard way.

I DREADED GOING TO MY sales job in the morning. The alarm would sound and I'd lie there, counting all the reasons I despised the job. I call it the time of the squeaky wheel in my life. The wheel was squeaking, demanding attention but I never gave it any. Jolted awake by that confounded mechanical noisemaker on my nightstand I'd turn on the TV and get my daily beating of news as I wolfed down a slice of toast. Jumping in the car I'd strap on my protective gear for the race to work, constantly calculating road closings and weather conditions, and jockeying for position in traffic. A myriad of electronic gadgets kept my day running at optimal level for peak performance, requiring the least amount of personal interaction with my clients and coworkers. I spent four to five hours in the confines of my cubicle walls before wolfing down my second meal of the day in the allotted thirty-minute limit, constantly thinking about the accounts I needed to contact after lunch. The day was often interrupted with meetings or a spreadsheet of sales calculations reminding all of us that the clock was tick-tocking away and we needed to work harder.

I had two superiors; for the sake of description I'll just call them the Fat Man and the Skinny Man. The Fat Man was one step above the Skinny Man on the corporate ladder and during my time in the department he said at least five times that he had "licked anorexia a long time ago." The Fat Man said all salespeople needed to be at their desks, phone to their ears at 8 A.M. sharp. It made no difference that my accounts were all on the West Coast and were still sleeping when I arrived at work. The Skinny Man then patrolled the sales floor to make sure said phones were up to said salespeople's ears. The Skinny Man liked to use phrases like, "okey-dokey, artichokey" or "Later, gator" and

"Isn't that a coinkidink?" One morning, I dropped off my things at my desk and stepped into the restroom. I arrived at my desk at roughly 8:03 or 8:04. The Skinny Man said, "Where have you been?"

"In the restroom," I said, sinking into my gray uphol-stered chair. "I dropped off my things and then ran down the hall to the bathroom."

The Skinny Man's brows furrowed into a tight V. "We really need you at your desk at eight o'clock," he said, whispering, almost pleading. The Fat Man waddled out-side my cubicle wall and rested his puffy face on top of it, awaiting possible crisis intervention. I looked at my purse and jacket. Didn't they prove I was in the building? The look on the Skinny Man's pointed face told me that my "things" couldn't make phone calls to my sleeping West Coast accounts. He looked across the aisle to Lucinda's station. She'd already been there an hour and a half mak-ing calls to her East Coast accounts. She got up every day at 4:00, dropped her husband off at work, and drove across town to be at her cubicle at 6:30. She talked too loud and laughed even louder. The Skinny Man raised the corners of his mouth in an aw-shucks-can't-you-read-between-the-lines kind of way. *She's already logged ninety minutes and you're three minutes late. Don't make me come out and say it.*

"Sorry about that," I said, shoving my things beneath my desk. The Skinny Man smiled and the Fat Man shuffled away to put out another "fire."

At day's end I merged back into traffic for the race home so I could wake up and do it all over again the next day. It was a complacent and routine existence and it left little room to really enjoy life. I was the hamster on the wheel and it was obvious that, unlike Lucinda, I could not hear the language of sales. As Jack Nicholson said in the movie of the same name I thought, "Is this as good as it gets?" The beauty of grace says no. There's more.

There's more love after the infidelity, more joy after the bankruptcy, more than just scars from the divorce, more fulfillment after the failed business venture, more than the pain of abuse, more life than the endless monotony of the job. Providence continuously spoke into my life; I just failed to see or hear, begrudging the tedium of my life. But I wonder if it isn't the ordinary that brings focus to our lives? Isn't it in the humdrum, boredom, and the daily minutia that we discover what we like and dislike as well as our gifts and weaknesses? In the ticktock passing of time our life speaks to us, revealing who we are, but it's up to us to rummage around and discover what it's saying.

Writing work continued to flow my way yet I stayed locked in a job that was unrewarding. I wanted out . . . but then I got pregnant.

I WAS SICK EVERY DAY. I'd wake up and vomit, pass someone wearing perfume in the halls at work and dash inside the bathroom to vomit; I'd walk Bailey, our miniature schnauzer, around the neighborhood and stop and vomit in someone's yard. It got to the point where the neighbors said, "Grab the hose, Harry. Here comes that rude woman who always vomits in our yard." For a week straight I thought I had a virus. Morning sickness lasted all day long, which was inconvenient at work. One afternoon I ate my lunch and after I walked up the stairs to the sales department I felt a wave of nausea. I ran to the bathroom and made it back to my desk six minutes late. The Skinny Man was not pleased.

"Is something wrong?" he asked.

"I don't feel well today," I said.

"Well, isn't that a coinkidink because you've been absent from your desk a lot this *week*." He emphasized *week* for my sake, just in case I thought it was just today that was the problem.

The Skinny Man was getting under my skin. "I know. I haven't felt well this week."

He leaned in close. "There's a huge sales frontier out there that needs discovering." I felt grinding nausea deep in my stomach. Did he just use the term *sales frontier?* "It could just be me but you don't seem committed to discovering what's out there. Do you need to go talk to the Fat Man?" I shook my head. I think I would have quit that day but if my hunch was right and I was pregnant then I'd need the job till the baby came. "Now," the Skinny Man said, puffing his chest out to the size of a chicken, "are you committed?" I nodded. I loved my clients but calling them ad nauseam had left me dry. "Are we okey-dokey?" I smiled and picked up my phone. He clapped me on the back and squeezed my shoulder. "Later, gator."

At the end of that week I realized the nausea I had was entirely different from any virus. Any woman who's ever experienced pregnancy understands there's no real way to describe the nausea. It sort of feels like your stomach has turned inside out and someone is pulling it up through your throat. One afternoon I took a pregnancy test when

Troy wasn't home. Four years into our marriage, I was going to be a mother.

TROY WAS AN A&R (artist and repertoire) director of a record company. He signed new talent and oversaw the production of their albums. On the evening I found out I was pregnant, he was on his way out the door for a long night in the studio with NewSong, one of the bands he worked with, and asked me to come along. I didn't feel well but Troy was adamant. "It'll be fun," he said. I couldn't imagine being up till the wee hours of morning. It was six o'clock and I was ready for bed! It wasn't the way I wanted to tell him but he insisted I come along. I grabbed the camera and took his picture when I told him I was pregnant. His mother once said he was born smiling, but on that day it was electric.

The nausea and the vomiting never stopped. Oh sure, the doctor gave me some meds to help prevent the nausea but there was that slim percentage of patients who never feel any relief. I was one of those patients. While riding to church one Sunday morning I grabbed the door handle and tried to open it. It was locked. "Are you going to throw up?" Troy asked, crossing lanes on the highway. I nodded and unlocked the door, attempting to open it but my seatbelt held me in place. "Don't throw up in the car," Troy yelled, darting through cars. "Hold it. Hold it! Don't vomit in the car," he said, pulling onto the side of the highway. I released my seatbelt and tumbled out of the car. Afterward, I sat back down in my seat and looked over at Troy. "That was a close one," he said. I stared at him. "You should really bring a bag wherever you go." I didn't respond. "You know. For the vomiting."

"Shut up," I said.

"No problem," he said, pulling back onto the highway.

For three months straight I was exhausted. Most women gain weight during their first trimester and I lost five pounds. When the clock rang in the morning I was too tired to pull myself out of bed, especially knowing where I was headed for five days out of the week. I didn't have a driving passion for sales and it seems that passion and desire are prerequisites to any calling in life. They are true gifts of grace. I didn't have a calling. I had a job, and I'm convinced a frustrating, unfulfilling job can be fatal to the human spirit. Over time my soul was making its desires known.

"You can find another job," Troy told me repeatedly.

"Who's going to want to hire me for six months knowing I'll need time off for the baby? I can't do that."

"Plenty of places would hire you."

I shook my head. "No. The jobs I'd be able to find would be something in retail or a restaurant, and you know they won't pay what I'm making now."

"Who cares?! At least you'd be happy for six months while you're at work."

Good grief. He had an answer for everything but I was determined to stick it out till the end. That was the better plan.

WHEN I WAS FOURTEEN WEEKS along I woke up one morning and I wasn't sick anymore. I didn't throw up at all throughout the day. I woke up the next day and I wasn't sick again and I just knew that something was wrong. I went to work and had the phone to my ear at 8 A.M. when I felt I needed to rush to the bathroom. I dropped the phone, ran down the hall, and discovered I was bleeding. My heart started racing because I knew something was terribly wrong. I called Troy and told him I thought I should go to the doctor. I popped my head inside the Skinny Man's office. "I need to go to the doctor," I said. He didn't know what was wrong with me but he saw I didn't look well. He nodded and said he'd see me whenever I returned.

I met Troy at the doctor's office and the nurse led us to

a room where I lay down on the table while she moved the ultrasound wand over my abdomen. Troy and I watched the screen to see what she was staring at but didn't know what we were looking for. She stopped moving the wand and looked at me. "Donna, there's no heartbeat here. I'm so sorry but you've lost the baby."

I cried all the way home. We rented every comedy we could think of and I cried through all of them. Three days later when the doctor performed a D&C I cried all the way home again.

Four weeks later I lost my job.

F I V E

God prescribes, carves out, calculates and arranges every-
thing for us, and thus explains His will.

—JOHANN SEBASTIAN BACH, COMPOSER

THE SALES FRONTIER WAS BIG but so was our sales force and
two people had to go. I wasn't born to be in sales. Some
people are. God was busy carving out and arranging things
in my life but I was too frustrated to detect any of his work.
But without frustration and disappointment I don't know
how he would ever get some of us to do anything.

At a follow-up appointment to the gynecologist a few
months later I was flipping through stacks of magazines in
her office and read a quote from Simone Weil, a French
philosopher and activist, who said, "Each thing that takes
place, whether it be fortunate, unfortunate, or unimportant

from our particular point of view, is a caress of God's."
That caress is grace at the end of our rope.

Troy received a call from our old college friends Bob
and Dannah Gresh. They needed help with a mainstream
radio station in Missouri, outside of St. Louis, and asked if
we'd come help them get it off the ground. I didn't want to
move. I loved Nashville and had no desire to move to a
small town. We talked over the pros and cons, made a
couple of trips to Missouri and ultimately decided in 1995
to pack up and move. We sold a lot of our things and
moved the rest into a two-bedroom duplex. Troy was
tapped to help handle the administrative aspects of the radio station, and I would write and produce commercials and
read the news for the morning show.

The town was small and came with several people
who were obliged to believe that if you hadn't been born
and raised within the county then you had no business living there whatsoever. A professional actor's theater took
up residence inside an old church and put on several productions a year. Despite a lukewarm embrace from some
citizens of the town I was eager about the possibility of
helping with the theater.

It was fun and exciting getting the station up and running but a year-and-a-half later I still wasn't pregnant. My

doctor put me on Clomid, a pill to help induce ovulation. I took it for six months without any success. A month went by, maybe two, before I saw my doctor again. He suggested I sit down with a noted fertility specialist in St. Louis. By the time I made the appointment and finally got in to see him it had been two-and-a-half years since I lost the baby.

Troy and I took the morning off from work and traveled to St. Louis. When we arrived on the eighth floor of the medical center there was only one other woman sitting in the waiting room. I filled out the book-length questionnaire while Troy flipped through magazines. We were still wait-ing an hour later and had long grown bored with the maga-zines when Troy said, "What's taking so long? Is a woman giving birth back there?" The other woman laughed and rolled her eyes in agreement. When a nurse came for her I gave her a nod of congratulations. The nurse left us sitting without a word. "They're a friendly bunch, aren't they?" Troy said. Thirty minutes later the nurse came for us and led us into the doctor's office. We chatted through the im-portant points: miscarriage, Clomid, and lack of pregnancy before she said, "He'll be right in."

Fifteen minutes later we were still waiting. I had cleaned out my purse a couple of times and Troy took a nap. A dark, curly-haired doctor whisked in several minutes later, arousing Troy to an upright, hand-extended position. The doctor sat behind his relatively clean desk—so clean in fact it didn't even include our file—and folded his hands. Without a word of small talk he got right down to it. "So, you lost a baby how long ago?"

"It's been two-and-a-half years," I said.

"How long on Clomid?"

"Six months."

"You're how old?"

"Thirty."

A few questions later he said, "You have a ten-percent chance of having children."

I felt my heart drop. How could he say that without looking at my file? Where *was* my file? Don't doctors take some sort of bedside-manner class in medical school? If so, *how* did he pass? Shouldn't he test us or something before dropping a bomb in our lap? Shouldn't he at least address me by my name?

"There are lots of things we can try," he said. "First, we can see if your husband's sperm can penetrate hamster eggs." I didn't hear a word after that and if memory serves, Troy passed out. We went to lunch, I don't remember where, and I cried through the entire meal. My childhood dreams were so simple. I thought, *Didn't you get that memo? Didn't you get any of those memos over the years?* At the time, there was a sixteen-year-old pregnant in our church. In the last several months we had watched her belly grow and her relationship sour with the teenage father. As her stomach expanded she was rooting on the high school football team and doing homework sitting on her twin-sized canopied bed while Troy and I were on the cusp of experimenting with hamster eggs and sperm. The logic of that was upside down.

We never really forget anything, it seems. Our body, mind, and spirit just store our secrets away in a deep and hidden place until a smell, a sound, a touch, or a doctor's lack of kindness ushers us into the darkness. I sat inside that crowded restaurant and was back inside Kevin Taylor's bedroom. I thought of what happened and all the things I wish I'd done to stop it; I thought of the doubts and the shame and the guilt that I could never forgive myself for; I thought of steeling myself against the world with clinched fists as I set out to prove that I could make it on my own. In my heart I just *knew* that what happened was the reason I couldn't have children. I questioned God's wisdom in standing by in silence as pain continued to plague the world and wondered, if the Kingdom of God is within us, why he literally didn't kick the hell out of molesters like Kevin Taylor, or the man who, that morning, had dropped his baby onto his head from a second-story window, or the woman who left her three small children abandoned and starving inside her dilapidated home. Although my problems seemed minor compared to what was on the daily news I wondered how an all-powerful and all-loving God could allow the headlines to play out day after day. Herman Melville said in a letter, "The reason the mass of men fear God, and at bottom dislike Him, is because they rather distrust His heart, and fancy Him all brain . . ." In a world that spun more inside out than right side up I had a tremendous distrust of God's heart.

I didn't touch my food. Tears streamed down my face throughout the meal and Troy finally said, "Are you going to eat those fries, because you're just ruining them." I laughed and then cried harder, wiping my face with a napkin. Troy glanced to the people around us. "I wish you'd stop crying before all these people think I'm a wife beater." I laughed. "That's it," he said. "More laughing and less crying." A thin line separates joy and sorrow, and in a blink more tears streamed down my face. Troy leaned over the table and took hold of my hand. "This means we can adopt children. I've always wanted to adopt and this gives us every reason to do it."

I shook my head. "We'll never be able to say, 'Oh look,

she's got your eyes and my nose,' or 'He looks just like my mother's baby picture but has my father's forehead.'"

"But we'll never notice any of that," Troy said. "Have you ever heard a mother brag about the beauty of her homely child? Parents see beauty, nothing else. We'll never notice that our kids don't look like us." I nodded but couldn't agree with him. I was certain that every time I looked at my child that I'd know he or she wasn't really mine.

PRIOR TO THAT FIRST APPOINTMENT Troy and I had moved into a three-bedroom home. A creek ran behind the house and we discovered that part of the lot was in a flood zone, but the Realtor pointed out how far the creek was from the house and really, it would take a *lot* of rain to get the creek to overflow. We decided to put up a picket fence for Bailey much like the one we had at our Nashville home. We had no idea how much it would rain in Missouri or how many times we would *keep* putting up that same fence! We changed the mantra of "when it rains, it pours" to "when it rains, it always takes out our fence."

There's a point in everybody's life when the wheels come off; for me they came off in Missouri and I found myself stranded in the desert, wandering around in the dust of broken dreams. I was emotionally and spiritually barren; if anything could go wrong it did (we mended the fence three times in our first eight months in the home), and God was noticeably absent during all of it. I felt forgotten and ignored. In the desert we want to know that Someone knows that we're nomadic and drifting but there seems to be no sense of concern. I went to church each Sunday hoping that something would be said that would help. I could have stopped going altogether; that would have been the easy thing to do but I wanted to hear *something*.

One Sunday I followed along as the minister read from the Bible that love always protects, always trusts, always hopes, and always perseveres. I sighed. If that was the case then I lacked *that kind* of love and it seemed God did as well. I prayed that he would fix my body and fix Troy's body but the doors of Heaven felt closed. Desert years can be brought on by anything and the desert can be found anywhere from a row house in Detroit, a movie studio in Los Angeles, a new job in Paris, a cattle ranch in Texas, or a college campus in New York. Where is God in the desert? He seems silent, hidden, and indifferent, and the windows of Heaven feel battened down. Sadness turns to disappointment and then into complete and total bitterness.

In the desert we look back on former days and even if they stunk we think, "I was happy then." Throughout our lives we have always maintained the same code. We assume that if we have a "dignified" job, obey the law, stay out of jail, and pay our taxes on time that we're entitled to some small corner of happiness. We believe that if we're kind to clerks and waitresses, throw a few dollars to the homeless, and back a worthy cause that God, like some mystical, omniscient Santa, will keep the presents coming. But one day the presents stop coming and happiness as we have defined it is a faded recollection. People who don't believe in God expect nothing of him so are presumably never upset or disappointed with him but for those of us who see his hand on this world in the oceans and stars and in the faces of our neighbors, we expect something, *anything*, that whispers to us that there is some sort of road map for our life. All of these expectations languish in the desert years. It's difficult to agree with Wolfgang Amadeus Mozart and "submit steadfastly to the Divine will, fully convinced it will be for our good, for he does all things well." In the middle of my sadness and complete disappointment no one, not even Mozart, could have convinced me that broken dreams could be for my own good.

My doctor recommended our seeing another fertility specialist in St. Louis; it took two months to get an appointment. We drove into the city again and a nurse led us to the doctor's office filled with dark leather furniture and paintings on the walls. On the bookshelves behind the desk were several pictures and models of male and female reproductive organs. Troy shuddered, looking at the shiny, plastic organs. "I *really* hope he's not going to pull any of those down." We were greeted by a warm, friendly physician who sat on the edge of his desk as he talked in length with us about our medical history.

He flipped through our file and looked at me over his glasses. "How young are you?" he asked. I smiled. I was really going to like this doctor. He outlined a series of tests he wanted to do that day and to Troy's delight he retrieved the models of the fallopian tubes and ovaries from the bookshelf and held them in front of Troy's face. He explained that one third of infertility causes can be traced to women, one third to men, and the remaining third is undetermined. Before leaving that day we left a nurse with several vials of blood, and I had an ultrasound. A couple of weeks later the doctor recommended I have a test performed at our local hospital. Technicians would inject dye, which shows up as blue on an X-ray, into my uterus to check for physical problems and to see if the dye moved normally through the uterus into the fallopian tubes, or if there were blockages that prevented an egg from moving from the fallopian tube to the uterus.

I wore the required gown and nothing else, and my teeth chattered as I entered a room cold enough to hang meat. "Well, hello there," I heard a man say. I turned and saw a man from our church dressed in green scrubs. "I didn't realize you were our patient today."

"Heeyy," I stammered, looking for the best place to make a new door. "I didn't know you worked here." I felt a breeze and held my gown tight around my back. "What are the odds that you'd work *here*, doing *this?*" I backed up toward the wall. There was no way, just no way I was going to lie there with my feet up in stirrups while this man I passed in the church halls pumped my fallopian tubes full of blue dye. A Rolodex of ways to excuse myself flipped through my brain.

A man dressed in a white jacket walked through the door beside me and turned to see me shivering against the wall. He introduced himself as the doctor and explained that he'd be performing the procedure. I exaggerated a sigh of relief and swiped my hand over my brow. My church friend laughed and said I'd lie on the table and they'd pull a curtain over me that would hang above my waist. On one side of the curtain the doctor would inject the dye while my church buddy and I watched what was happening on a TV screen by my head on the other side of the curtain (still awkward but at least he was on the head side of the curtain!). The results of that test were sent to St. Louis and after all our initial series of tests, Troy and I fell into that final undetermined category for the cause of infertility.

It was raining when I left the hospital. I ran for my car and drove through town to work. I felt dejected and lonely in this town, and to be honest, unlike college, I was having a hard time enjoying being in the same space with Troy and he felt the same way about me. The financial and emotional stress of our circumstances was making me miserable and I began to hate every aspect of our life. There were no parking spots available on the street so I had to park in the lot at the end of the road and make a dash for the front door. A well-meaning friend saw me park my car and met me at the front of the radio station, under the awning. Her young sons were with her. She handed me a book about coping with infertility. For this very reason Troy and I had told few people about our circumstances.

"I thought you might like to read this," she said. I was not in the mood for this. I wanted to hand back the book to her but I smiled and thanked her with as much enthusi-asm as I could muster. "I have a friend who's also been through several infertility procedures. Maybe you'd like to talk to her."

Nothing in me wanted to talk to her friend. "I don't know," I said. "Our doctor's been really good about an-swering all our questions."

Her son reached out his hand and let the water from the awning pour between his fingers. She grabbed his arm before he bolted into the street. "But doctors don't know what it's like emotionally. My friend does. I think she'd be very encouraging." I *really* didn't want to talk to her friend. "She even lives in St. Louis so the next time you're there maybe you could just meet her for lunch and talk." Why couldn't I just tell her that I didn't want to talk to her any longer *or* her friend? "You know what? It'd probably be eas-ier if she just called you. She could give you a word or two of encouragement. Do you want me to have her call you?"

No, I screamed on the inside. *I don't want to talk to her.* "Sure," I said. I watched her two boys run into her legs as they chased each other on the sidewalk in front of the radio station.

"You know, if nothing works out, you can always adopt," she said.

I thought, *That's so easy for you to say with your two children climbing up your legs. Just shut up and stop smiling.* I smiled and took the book without ever reading a word.

Early that evening her friend called to offer "a word or two of encouragement." She was a fast-talker and her voice was tense with passion. "They never tell you about all the side effects of those medications," she said. "It could be years before my body is stripped of all their harmful effects . . . or maybe never." I sat on the floor in the bedroom. This was going to be a looonng conversation. She took another breath. "We stopped all treatments over a year ago. I mean, I just can't keep pumping this stuff into my system and we absolutely do *not* want to adopt. I mean, what if we get a child whose mother was addicted to crack or a baby with fetal alcohol syndrome?" I opened my mouth to say something, but she continued. "And do you know how much money it takes to adopt? We're already tapped out from all the treatments. Who has money to adopt after fertility specialists make you jump through all their hoops? It's a racket! I think it needs to be government regulated." I wondered if she'd notice if I just hung up the phone. She blathered for nearly thirty minutes till I couldn't take another word of encouragement. I told her I had to go, and as she sucked in air for more verbal volley I thanked her quickly and hung up the phone.

Troy had been waiting for my conversation to end and called me to the kitchen. He was standing at the patio doors videotaping the rushing water in our backyard. We even called our friend Paul to watch it with us. A child's bright blue bucket rushed past us along with a red plastic rake. We watched as the back corner of the fence gave way and floated down the creek. It was the perfect way to end the day.

EARLIER IN THE YEAR I realized I had a difficult time walking down the hallway at work without feeling tipsy. If I stood up too fast I got lightheaded but one of the scariest symptoms was feeling panicked and nauseous if I drove over a body of water. My family physician diagnosed it as vertigo, an inner-ear imbalance. "Is it triggered by my allergies?" I asked.

"Could be. I have some patients who experience it throughout a sinus infection because everything up here is congested," she said, placing her fingers on the side of her nose. "Your case isn't life threatening, just annoying, but I strongly urge you to talk with me or your fertility doctor about medications to make sure they don't worsen the dizziness."

Our fertility specialist recommended that we try follicle-stimulating hormone injections (FSH) and assured me that it wouldn't worsen my vertigo. FSH reminds the ovaries to begin the process of ovulation. I was supposed to give myself the shot in my thigh, but fortunately I lived close enough to my local doctor that he said his nurse would give me the daily injections. Neither Troy nor I had any idea how much the medicine would cost but assumed our insurance wouldn't cover it; we were right and the cost was almost as much as our mortgage. Troy and I prayed that the shots would work and that I'd get pregnant. I didn't. I repeated the shots the following month, also without success, and it felt like a black cloud swallowed our home. I was sick and tired of the process, the town, the job, and my husband. There were many times I felt it was his fault that we were in Missouri in the first place. The desert was getting drier by the day.

The specialist recommended we try intrauterine insemination (IUI), a procedure where they'd deposit Troy's sperm directly into my uterus through a catheter. (It is as sterile and clinical as it sounds.) I was discouraged by the possibility of yet another expensive procedure. Days later

I became ill; my joints ached for two weeks straight. I made an appointment with our family physician. Ironically, she was out sick and I saw the new practitioner, a young woman who looked fresh out of medical school.

After examining me she said, "I saw you in *Steel Magnolias*." We talked about the production and my involvement in the theater. "Anything coming up next?"

"I'm writing a production for a dinner theater fundraiser in the fall."

She nodded. "I heard you on the radio last night at the gas station and then again this morning. How many hours do you work?"

I shrugged. "It depends. Fifty. Sometimes sixty."

"And you work with the theater and are driving to St. Louis for infertility treatments." She sat in a chair by the door and wrapped her hands around a knee. "Our body is designed in such a way that parts of it will shut down if we don't listen to what it's saying." I looked at her. "Your body is going through a lot. Not just with the hours you work but the mental, physical, and emotional stress you're going through with infertility. You have a virus but it's not going to go away unless your body gets some rest."

"From the treatments?" I asked.

She nodded. "I think that'd be a good idea for a couple

of months. And if there's any way you can reduce your hours at work it would relieve a lot of stress in your body, and the pain will go away in your joints."

I left her office more discouraged than ever. Nothing good had come out of our move to Missouri: We were ninety miles from our fertility specialist, the treatments were expensive; I had thought the professional theater would be a creative outlet but the theater's director was, in my opinion, an egotist and difficult to work with; the work at the radio station had become all-consuming; the long hours and fiscal turbulence of the business had fractured our friendship with Bob and Dannah; a financial and emotional strain squeezed Troy and me dry; and God was far away.

A couple of Sundays later I went to church and prayed that something in the minister's message would offer encouragement. I opened the church bulletin and read the dates of four upcoming baby showers. My eyes filled and I put the bulletin on the pew beside me. I knew our names would never be listed there. I knew people would never stop me in the hall and pat my pregnant belly when they asked me how far along I was. I knew no one would ever look at the squirming baby in my arms and say, "She has your eyes doesn't she? But those are her daddy's ears!" I could hear people chatting and laughing around me but I was as lonely as I'd ever been.

In the weeks to come we discovered there were two teenagers pregnant in our community. The reality of it slapped me hard; children could get pregnant but we couldn't. I had a real problem with God concerning that. Over and over we hear the same stories of children getting pregnant while couples who can actually provide for children couldn't have them. I was tired of the struggle and fed up with all of it. My friend David Knight has always said, "If you can stand the pull, God will pull you through." I was sick and tired of the pulling and pushing and the effort to breathe. I really felt as if I'd bottomed out in Missouri and became so angry at God's lack of concern and the distance he was keeping that I flipped open my Bible in anger. I thought, *I know there are promises in here about a happy home and that whole thing about a full quiver is somewhere and I'm going to find those promises and throw them in your face.*

That act was the crack through which grace slipped in.

S I X

Nothing is discovered without God's intention and assis-
tance.

—CHARLES DICKENS, AUTHOR

THE MYSTERIOUS YET WONDERFUL ATTRIBUTE of grace is that it is never earned or deserved, and it will never be forced upon anyone—it can only be received. At some point we have to say, "I'm sick of just hoping for the best and want something else, something life-altering." I was exhausted from roaming the desert in Missouri and each day I opened the Bible with a heated attitude that said, Show me *something*.

I began reading helter-skelter, flipping from the New to the Old Testament. I read about the Israelites and their own wanderings in the wilderness. Creation led them out of hard slavery in Egypt and they complained with every step of freedom they took. They defied, denied, and rejected God with each dusty mile they traveled. As they ranted and raved and shook their fists, Isaiah wrote of The Creator's feelings toward them and said, "In all their distress he, too, was distressed."

Poet William Blake said if God is anything he is understanding. God cared and tried time and again to show the Israelites that. He freed them from slavery, promised them a land of their own, even fed and clothed them, but they found fault with him at every bump along the trip. What's interesting is that God never strong-armed them into submission. He didn't paralyze them when they built a golden calf to worship, or send them packing back to slavery in Egypt when they had the audacity to say they'd be better off there, or close the breadline when they complained about eating manna "again," but instead allowed them to grumble and carp and rail against him. I thought it was interesting that from the beginning of time and through centuries of man's inhumanity to man, God had never subjected us to his all-consuming power. With one tip of the earth's axis we could be obliterated in an instant. He had instead chosen the painstaking way of love, breaking through the chinks of our heart with small taps of grace. At some point (it was certainly no great epiphany but just a common moment during an ordinary day) I realized the Israelites had turned away, not God. For years he had held out his hand to them saying, "Here, here, here," but it was impossible to receive a gift when their backs were turned to the giver. It was a fascinating story and in a fleeting moment I wondered if I was like that. No, no. That couldn't be me. I still went to church, for crying out loud. I put it out of my mind and went to bed.

WITHIN THREE MONTHS I HAD stopped working at the radio station. Any passion I had to wake up at 4:30 for my air shift had leeched away in the previous months. Troy and I had been sensing that our work was finished at the station and after my conversation with the doctor about slowing down, it seemed like the time was right to move on. The school district was in need of substitutes and after talking with someone in the superintendent's office I learned that I could take on as much work as I wanted or turn it down, it was up to me. In January 1999, Troy phased out of his job at the station as well. We both knew it was time to move. For two months he looked for something to help pay the bills as he sent résumés out to Nashville because small towns are rarely bustling with job opportunities. We held garage sales in anticipation of moving somewhere (*anywhere*) and Troy sold his motorcycle to help pay the bills, but no work became available. We kept the heat at sixty-two degrees and bundled up in the house to keep our electric bill low. Both of us prayed that a job would open for Troy but nothing happened. We were getting used to praying without any answers. We were running out of options. We couldn't pay our bills on a substitute teacher's salary. We could sell the house and move but where would we go without a job lined up? My friend Chris Carter said, "Sometimes God's not calling you to move on. He's calling you to camp out." But I was tired of camping out and angry at God's wearisome pace and lack of direction.

Before turning the light out one night I read in the book of Jeremiah, "For I know the plans I have for you," declares the Lord, "plans to prosper you and not to harm you, plans to give you hope and a future." *Really?* I thought. *If you know them then why don't you show them?* I wondered how many people ever really discovered God's plan for their life. There were a lot of promises in that statement with plans to prosper, the promise not to harm, the promise of hope, and the plan of a future, but it felt like they would demand the maximum of faith on my part. I wanted something like "CliffsNotes" faith that would give me all the answers without the work. We all come to a crossroads;

most of us will have several in a lifetime, and when we feel the doors to heaven are constantly barricaded at those crossroads we face two choices: We either turn from God or we camp out for a while.

I flipped back through the pages and landed in Genesis. (I had no rhyme or reason for the way I shuffled through the books and I don't recommend starting at the beginning. My friend Anita Pringle always tells new readers to start at the back of the Bible in First John, then to the Gospel of John because both books are all about love. "Who doesn't need more love?" she says.) I read about Jacob, who was one of Israel's patriarchs as well as a schemer, a manipulator, and a first-class mama's boy. For years Jacob worked to earn the hand of his one true love, then wrestled with God and lived to tell his grandchildren about it. Jacob's life was a mess from the moment he entered the scene with his twin brother Esau. Dysfunctional is much too mild a word to describe his screwed-up childhood. He cheats Esau of his birthright as the eldest son and is then on the run for much of his life until he meets her—Rachel. She's lovely and soft and just what his wandering soul needs but her father tells Jacob he'll have to work seven years to earn her hand. Jacob does so and on his wedding night discovers his father-in-law has tricked him and he has married Rachel's spinster older sister, Leah. It's a sad story for all involved. Rachel is heartbroken, Jacob is incensed, and Leah always knows she isn't loved.

Over twenty years later, in chapter 32, Jacob has had enough and wants to go home and face his twin brother and right the wrong he did to him. With his family in tow (he ended up marrying Rachel), he camps out alongside a river, hoping for a little rest along the journey. He's nervy and restless and his mind is racing. In the pitch of night he hears something that is more than the rush of the river and realizes he's not alone. He spins on his heels straining to see. Is it Esau? Someone grabs him and pins him to the ground. An intense wrestling match ensues but without the unsightly uniforms. Jacob's opponent is strong, fast, and agile. The fight rages for hours, leaving Jacob sore, bloody, exhausted, and covered in dirt and mud. Finally, his opponent touches Jacob's leg, dislocating his hip. Pain shoots through Jacob's body and he staggers about, flailing his arms for balance then wraps them around his attacker.

"Let me go, for it is daybreak," the stranger said.

Jacob held on tighter. "I will not let you go unless you bless me."

Then the man said, "Your name will no longer be Jacob, but Israel, because you have struggled with God and with men and have overcome." And he blessed him there. After years of brawling, scheming, and running Jacob camped out for a while and received the Holy blessing. It's an intriguing story about an ordinary man who went head to head with God. He ran, fought, and struggled for most of his life but in the end he would have rather been hobbled than turn his back on God forever.

I had been wrestling with God for years in my own way. I rummaged through the drawer in my nightstand and found a pen, writing the words, *Bless me* in the margin next to Jacob's story. In the end, our eyes may not see it, our ears may not hear it, or our hands may not touch it, but it's what our souls want and cry out for in the darkness. *Bless me! Not because of who I am or what I have or haven't done but because of who you are! Bless me with your grace. Bless me with your mercy. Bless me!* It's in those excruciating, dark, and raw moments that we feel God . . . maybe for the first time in our lives. It wasn't momentous; the sheets didn't ruffle and a shaft of light didn't fill the room but as I rolled over to fall asleep I seemed to sense that God *was* blessing me. I just didn't understand how.

IN THE SPRING OF '99 Troy's brother Todd called from Alaska. He needed help building his house and wondered if Troy was interested in the work. He'd be gone a little over a month. It wasn't ideal but Troy could visit with Todd and his wife, Mary, and continue to send out résumés. Due to my tenacious virus and the financial strain of fertility procedures we had stopped going to the specialist indefinitely so it made sense for Troy to go.

The substitute work kept me occupied but that month lasted a year as I clunked around our house, packing or throwing away things in the hope of moving on. I was alone in a town that was no longer home and it often felt as if the walls were closing in on me. After Troy's first week in Alaska I went to the video store one day after work and rented *Chariots of Fire,* the four-time Academy Award–winning film about Eric Liddell, the gold-medal runner from the 1924 Paris Olympics. Eric had been born in China, the son of Scottish missionaries there. It was his desire to return to China after college to continue missionary work but there was a little event called the Olympics that he needed to compete in first. His sister Jenny was not pleased with his decision and told him with all the female politeness the 1920s demanded of women that he was missing his noble call in China and was a fool for participating in the games. Eric turned to his sister and said in his rich, Scottish brogue, "I know that God made me for a purpose. For China. But he also made me fast. And when I run I feel his pleasure. To give it up would be to hold him in contempt." Up to this point I had found the film to be rather slow-moving and boring but when I heard these words I grabbed the remote and rewound the tape. "When I run I feel his pleasure." I rewound it again. "When I run I feel his pleasure." These seven words popped off the screen in bold, emotional color. They were affecting and piercing because I didn't know what that was like, to enjoy doing something so much that it felt as if the Creator himself was smiling when I did it. That simple line reflected my own interior wanderings and my desperation to know what on earth I was here for.

Providence is there in each moment, small or large, leaving us with the choice to recognize or not recognize him. For me, he was in the moment I watched that scene from *Chariots of Fire*. I believe he can use a stroke from DaVinci's brush, a melody from Bach, a lyric from Bono, a scene from *Les Misérables*, or direction from Spielberg to reach our hearts in a dialect that only we can understand.

I realize now that the eloquent, yet sometimes brutally honest language of the arts has a way of penetrating the deepest places of our soul. French neoclassical painter Jean-Auguste-Dominique Ingres said, "Do not believe that

you can produce anything of worth . . . without the eleva-
tion of the soul." I don't contend that all art carries such
a noble purpose but much can offer us a glimpse into
the landscape of our inner selves.

For me, those seven words from *Chariots of Fire* elevated
my soul and echoed words I had first heard at the church
in the heart of Brunswick when I read that God had special plans for me and had called me through his grace. I
was still lonely, discouraged, and frustrated with God but
those words from a movie became an oasis in a dry place.

Days later I was reading Isaiah again, this time chapter
43. "Forget the former things," God says, "Do not dwell on
the past. See, I am doing a new thing! Now it springs up; do
you not perceive it? I am making a way in the desert and
streams in the wasteland." In chapter 46 I read, "I have made
you and I will carry you; I will sustain you and I will rescue
you." For some reason the words leaped off the page and I
underlined them. There was no angelic chorus but I had the
slightest inclination that God was giving me yet another occasion to recognize him. It was a soft melodic note of grace.

THE PHONE RANG EARLY ONE morning and I assumed it
was the school system but after looking at the clock I realized it was too late for them to call me. It was my friend

Beth who often kept her infant grandson for her daughter, Lesa, who was a struggling single mother. "Donna," she said. "I'm sorry to bother you so early in the morning but I'm trying to find someone to watch Brennan today. We didn't know Lesa was coming into town for job interviews but I have to work so I can't watch him."

"Sure, bring him over anytime," I said.

Beth dropped off Brennan within thirty minutes and handed him to me. His blanket and his clothes smelled like smoke. "Lesa smokes around him," Beth said, kissing Brennan's head. "We hate it and always tell her how dangerous it is but she won't listen to us. I'm sorry he smells that way." She handed me his diaper bag. "He'll take a couple of naps. One around ten and then after lunch around one. You can just lay him on his blanket and he'll go to sleep." Her eyes filled with tears as she turned to go. The last several years had been a hard journey with her daughter.

"We'll do great," I said, encouraging her.

"I know," she said, a tear falling down her cheek. "I can't tell you how thankful I am leaving him with you because I know you'll be good to him."

I closed the door behind her and Brennan snuggled up against my shoulder. I sat in our swivel chair and he sat in my lap and played with coasters from the nearby side table.

He laughed at peek-a-boo and when I tapped his nose and made a honking sound. He played with his feet as I gave him his bottle and then lay quietly on his blanket for his nap. He cried when he woke and when I pushed open the bedroom door he smiled at me as if he couldn't wait to see me again. I picked him up and he snuggled against my shoulder, wrapping his tiny arms around me. I patted his back and the smell of stale cigarettes filled our small space together. He picked up his head and smiled, and in that brief, random moment my heart awakened to the whisper of something soulish. I really felt that I *could* love a child that hadn't been born from me. I don't know how to describe those few seconds, but Frederick Buechner wrote, ". . . in the last analysis all moments are key moments, and life itself is grace."

A FEW DAYS BEFORE TROY was supposed to come home our phone rang after I returned from work. It was our long-time friend Eddie Carswell from Atlanta. Troy had worked with Eddie and NewSong, the band he led, for years at the record company. Eddie is gregarious and kind-hearted and uses great Southern words like "washing powder" and "billfold." After a minute of small talk Eddie said, "Donna, what in the world are you people doing in Missouri?"

I laughed and said, "That is a *great* question!"

"Do you think I could talk Troy into coming back to Nashville and managing us?"

"I'm sure he'd love to hear from you," I said. "But he's in Alaska right now."

"Do they have phones in Alaska?" Eddie asked.

Grace, like rain, was beginning to fall in the desert.

S E V E N

It is invariably true, that God conceals Himself from
those who tempt Him, and manifests Himself to those who
seek Him.

—BLAISE PASCAL, FRENCH SCIENTIST, PHILOSOPHER,

AND MATHEMATICIAN

WE KNEW IT WOULD BE impossible to buy a home in
Nashville with another mortgage in Missouri but we made
several trips to search for one and to find office space for
Troy. After several days of house hunting our Realtor happened to see a two-bedroom condo pop up on the Multi
Listing System (MLS). We couldn't believe the price; it was
just a little over $80,000. The Realtor drove us to the west
side of Nashville where a line of people was quickly parad-
ing in and out the condo's front door. That price had at-
tracted the attention of *a lot* of people. They were streaming

into the condo like ants so we jumped out of the car and hustled to the front door. As we approached the door we knew why everyone was moving at such a quick pace. The place was a dump. Actually, dumps would be ashamed to attach their good name to this condo. The owner had a dog who used the place as his personal toilet; there were bugs in the refrigerator, some layer of goo on the kitchen counter that held our Realtor's sleeve fast to it, smoke scum on the windows and walls, and garbage piled in every room. It was a feast for the eyes and nose. Troy's parents were visiting us from Alaska and in an act of grace they said they'd loan us the money for the condo until we could pay them back. We made an offer on it that day.

Troy's parents rolled up their sleeves and together we hauled appliances to the dump, knocked out walls, ripped up floorboards, and tore out the carpet. The carpet smelled so bad that even Bailey wouldn't sit on it. He just stood on it and stared at me like, "Are you kidding me? We're living here?" We slept on an air mattress while we did the initial work and once we had the place stripped down and cleaned we wore special masks to apply a layer of primer that killed odors trapped inside the walls and floorboards. We painted the walls and brought in new appliances, carpet, and a heat and air-conditioning unit that actually worked before heading back to Missouri for our things. That was August 1999.

We took a day to pack the moving truck and trailer, and planned to head to Nashville the next day, Sunday morning. Tornadoes had touched down in Nashville and a huge storm system was making its way across the midwest. We put Bailey in the cab of the truck and Troy pulled onto the highway. We could see the storm coming toward us. Within minutes we were in a downpour that lasted hours. We drove out of one storm into another, just inching along; cars had slowed to forty miles per hour on the highway. At one point, visibility was so poor that Troy pulled off the highway onto a quiet side road. We waited till the storm let up and then looked for a spot to turn around and get back on the highway. The road went on for miles without a place to turn around. Troy finally saw a road and he turned onto it looking for a turn-around area. Our new road turned out to be a *really* long driveway flanked by cornfields on either side. Troy stopped at the end of the driveway and we both stared at the house through the rain. There was no place to turn around and it would be impossible to back down the driveway with the truck and trailer. A man ran out of the house holding a plastic garbage bag over his head. "I'm really sorry," Troy yelled over the rain. "I thought this was a road."

"It happens a lot," the man said.

"I'm not sure how I can turn this around," Troy said, looking at the field of corn outside his window. By this time the man's wife and children had joined him in the rain. His wife carried an umbrella and his children chose the natural approach. Troy looked at her and shouted above the rain and the truck engine. "We really messed up," he said. "I'm sorry."

She smiled and waved her hand in the air. "No big deal at all. The kids think it's awfully exciting."

"Pull up as far as you can this way," the man said, waving us toward the house. Troy pulled forward and stopped when the tires met the lawn. "It's okay," the man yelled. "Just come on."

"I'm going to wreck your yard," Troy yelled, sticking his head out the window.

"It's just grass," the man said, throwing the limp trash bag to the ground. The wife smiled and waved us forward.

It took thirty minutes for us to maneuver the truck and trailer through the man's yard and back onto his driveway. His wife and children stayed with us despite the rain, truck fumes, and flying mud. "I need to pay you for the damage I did to your lawn," Troy said.

"No, you don't," the man said. "I'm tellin' ya. It's just grass." Troy was about to say something when the man waved us on.

"You all drive safe," his wife yelled, smiling.

Tears filled my eyes as Troy drove back down the driveway. "What's wrong?" he asked.

"I don't know," I said. But maybe I did. Maybe I was finally noticing how the ordinary scenes around me were painted. Maybe I was beginning to recognize that tears are God's way of asking me to pay attention, not only to where I've been but to where I'm headed, reminding me of what is important and who I'm supposed to be. The man and his family were ordinary people living a simple life in the midwest. Hollywood would look at them, their home, and their life as being unmemorable, nothing dramatic or cinematic, but through my tears I saw the event as rain-soaked grace.

THE STORM WAS RELENTLESS. THE entire trip normally took six-and-a-half hours but after four hours on the road we weren't even halfway to Nashville. As we plodded along we listened to several news reports about the tornado damage in Nashville and surrounding areas so we knew we were driving home to a mess. An hour later the skies finally turned from inky gray to red. The storm was breaking. Troy asked if I would mind driving for a while and he pulled into the parking lot of a large convenient store. I ran inside to use the restroom and to gather up some snacks and water for my time behind the wheel. When I opened the truck door I saw Troy leaning against the passenger door, asleep. When I was a little girl there was a man in our church who suffered from narcolepsy. He could fall off anytime during the hymns but then rouse himself for the beginning of Preacher Powers's message, only to drift off again before the first point was made.

Troy suffers from vehicle narcolepsy. (It's not an actual condition but it should be.) Unless tornadic winds and rains are pummeling a vehicle, Troy soon becomes the sleepy victim of the vibration, sound, and movement of an automobile, but then again Troy can sleep anywhere at anytime. One night in bed I once asked him to teach me how to fall asleep as fast as he does. He said, "Well, first you relax your entire body." I tried to do just that but couldn't get comfortable. "Then you take a couple of deep breaths." And by the time he got to the second deep breath he was fast asleep, which I thought was rude. He's a terrible sleep coach!

I closed the door to the U-Haul and glanced over at him. He was snoring and Bailey was curled up next to him. I pulled the truck and trailer out onto the highway and had driven about three-quarters of a mile when I saw it. I didn't know the Golden Gate Bridge was in Missouri but there it was, looming painfully long in front of me. I didn't think my vertigo would let me cross the bridge but reasoned that sometimes bridges are mostly concrete walls, which keep me from seeing the water so they're no big deal. I drove onto the bridge and discovered it had been put together with string and wire. The water loomed below me and my head began to reel. I looked over at Troy and he was still sleeping. I didn't need to wake him; I could do this.

I realized that the view of the river below wasn't as bad on the driver's side so I reasoned that if I could get more concrete between the passenger side and the bridge that I'd be okay crossing it. I pulled the truck into the center of the bridge but it didn't help. My stomach churned as the river now jumped up on both sides of the truck. No one was behind me so I thought that if I could slow down to a speed that made my head feel safe that I could get the truck across the bridge. I slowed down to 50, 40, 30, 25 miles per hour. I felt the trailer shift side to side in the wind and my heart beat out of my chest. Troy continued to snore as my head spun around the cab of the truck. Bailey sat up and looked out the front window then to me. He was putting enormous pressure on me so I ignored him. I thought that maybe if I scrunched down in my seat that I wouldn't be able to see the water so I slinked farther and farther down until just my eyes peered over the steering wheel. I was going ten miles an hour and by this time there were several cars behind me. The ruthless honking indicated that every driver back there lacked empathy and patience with my situation. I found this to be rude and impolite and did what every driver in my shoes would do: start to sweat and feel like vomiting. A car entered on the far side of the bridge but after he drove several feet he realized there wasn't room for both him and me on the bridge so he stopped and backed off the bridge.

Looking back, I know it looked like a terrorist situation. "Yeah, there's a U-Haul truck and trailer stopped in the middle of the bridge. I can just see the driver's eyebrows. And it appears that the passenger is dead."

Now something at that point woke Troy. It could have been the sound of horns behind us or the lack of movement to keep him lulled into a deep slumber but I personally think God tapped him on the shoulder and said, "You really need to see this."

Troy leaned up and looked out his passenger window. His head snapped when he saw how much pavement was on his side of the truck. He quickly realized we weren't moving and he turned to me. "What are you doing?" he asked. For some reason, panic was in his voice. I couldn't answer him. "Donna," he said, his voice rising. "What are you—"

"Shhh," I said, staring at the road. "My head feels like I could careen off the side of this bridge."

Oddly, those words made Troy a bit edgy. His seatbelt whizzed past his head and he squeezed in close to me. "Let go of the wheel," he said, trying to grab it but I couldn't let go. "Donna, *let go* of the wheel," he shouted. I couldn't move; my knuckles were stretched white around the wheel. "Donna," he screamed louder. "Let go!" He pried away each of my fingers. "Take your hands off the wheel." He pushed me close to the door and squeezed in behind the wheel, driving over the bridge and onto the exit ramp at the end. I had been behind the wheel from one exit to the next, which was exactly one mile. Troy jumped out of the truck, stretched his arms, and said, "That mile is just what I needed to keep me going." For the remainder of the trip any silence was punctuated with the snorting, hard laughter that comes from real and ridiculous moments.

* * *

A FORMER WRITING CLIENT HEARD I was back in town and within weeks of moving back to Nashville I was independently employed. I jumped right back into writing audio projects for him and worked several months on scripts for a video he was producing for a company on Music Row. Once I was established with work and Troy and I were settled into the condo I knew it was time to find another fertility specialist. My longtime gynecologist recommended a clinic and I made an appointment with one of the physicians. After he examined me he said, "You need to have surgery."

I thought, "Of course I do. That's the problem. I've needed surgery all along but the other doctors didn't catch it. This will clear everything up now."

I had laparoscopic surgery and waited to get pregnant. Three months went by, then four without any results. Our surroundings had changed but our circumstances hadn't. I was still frustrated, angry and disappointed. "What's wrong?" I'd pray. "Why won't you fix it?" Another arrow shot off in the dark in my feeble effort to know something. Isn't that why we often pray? We want to *know* something, understand the reason, or see the outcome so we cobble together a few words and shoot them off in the dark again and again in an effort to know, and then we wait. And the answer *does* come but not always in the way our souls wished. There's no documented word from God that says he promised life without struggle or pain. This morning, before I sat down to write these few pages, I went to traffic court (40 in a 30 mph zone) and a twenty-something defendant pleaded before the judge, "Don't you think this is an unfair situation?" Without a moment's hesitation the judge said, "All of life is unfair, son." *Look at my situation,* we pray. *Isn't this unfair?* Yes, Eternity nods. Yes, it is. And sometimes, on a clear day, his words echo in our spirit: *I am with you. I will help you. I will rescue you*—and we believe. On cloudy days, days more like winter than summer, we shuffle about without giving an ear to him or taking the time to set our jaw to murmur a quick "God help me" and our belief wanes. I had known both summer and winter days.

I continued my haphazard reading of the Bible and had also begun reading about the lives of some of the greatest thinkers and artists throughout the ages like Leo Tolstoy, who lived a trouble-plagued yet celebrated life. The theme of life and death was reflected in many of his works but at the age of fifty his contemplations brought on a crises of faith that drove him into the four Books of the Gospel (Matthew, Mark, Luke, and John) to research the life of the

Palestinian Jew called The Christ who from his beginning in Bethlehem has received a lot of bad press, making it difficult to discern opinion and truth. Tolstoy came away from his studies a changed soul with a new philosophy. He said, "For life is life only when it is the carrying out of God's purpose. But by opposing Him, people deprive themselves of life, and at the same time, neither for one year, nor for one hour, can they delay the accomplishment of God's purpose." I questioned what prompted Tolstoy to write that and jotted the quote down in a random notebook. Over the next few months I would add countless quotes from amazing thinkers, artists, poets, authors, ministers, and the Bible.

Sometime later in Psalm 33:11 I read that, "The plans of the Lord stand firm forever." In Isaiah chapter 46 I read, "What I have planned, that will I do." I opened my notebook and jotted these verses beneath Tolstoy's quote, curious if they were the verses that prompted Tolstoy's reflections. It occurred to me that we are constantly running, morphing, flailing, spinning, and changing but God's plan for us stays the same. We believe the divorce, the affair, the accident, the disgrace, or the failing will disqualify us. "Look at this," we say. "Look at what I did." Or, "Look at what happened to me. Whatever you planned for my life isn't going to work and I need a new plan." But a new plan is contrary to God's nature. There has *never* been a Plan B. I believe that inside all of us we want to believe that we're here for some higher purpose than to just pay our bills before the undertaker collects his check but there's a stopgap somewhere—Is it in the soul? Our spirit? The heart?—that hinders our discovery, leaving us with an inexpressible feeling that something is missing. It's an intangible; we can't describe it. All we know is that something is *not right* beneath our skin. Could that inner "whatever" be the voice of Providence inviting us to know him? The emptiness says: *Come to me. I'll never betray you. I know you by name. I know the plans I have for you.* I ignored that restlessness, and unconvinced that God really did have a purpose for me, I continued to drive my own plan. After all, isn't that easier and more manageable than discerning the mystery of the soul?

MY PRAYERS FOR A BABY grew more desperate and urgent in Nashville. I continued to pray, "Fix my body. Fix Troy's body," but again it felt like the prayers stopped at the ceiling. Somewhere, I came across a quote from Harriet Beecher Stowe, the author of *Uncle Tom's Cabin,* who was contemplating prayer when she said, "I think the All Wise often thinks beyond the words of our prayers and gives us the real thing." I wrote it down in my notebook and wondered what the real thing was. I assumed that if the All Wise thought beyond our feeble piecing together of the alphabet then the real thing had to be something deeper, higher, or broader than what we could humanly ask for, something beyond our own plan and design. I scribbled "God's dream?" beside the quote and put it away.

I opened the Bible one morning before working on a writing assignment and read the story of a young man named Lazarus who lived with his two sisters. Lazarus grew ill; it doesn't say what he contracted but the sickness was life threatening. His sisters sent for their friend Jesus because they knew he could heal their brother. It was a good thought but that was their plan, their way. Jesus didn't come and their brother died. Surely, God saw their circumstances and heard their cries. Why didn't he do something? I knew the end of the story; I'd heard it countless times: After being dead four days Jesus commanded that Lazarus come out of the grave and in seconds a mummylike figure emerged, his grave clothes still wrapped around him. The thought occurred to me that the Creator's unresponsiveness to the situation was as if he was saying, "Hold on. I'm orchestrating something so incredible up here that you'll never believe it." In my notebook I wrote down something my friend Chris Carter said: "It is

predictable that God will take care of us. What's unpre-
dictable is how he will do it." Like Martha and Mary, I was
looking for something I could see and wrap my arms
around, something predictable and safe.

I don't know why but in the days following I went
back to the story of Lazarus, reading and listening for the
stories in those few short verses. When mourners inside
the home heard that Jesus was coming Mary stayed put,
settled in her grief, but Martha ran out to meet him. She
pointed out the obvious and said, "If you had been here
my brother would not have died." Then she said, "But."
My friend Ann Blackburn says the word *but* always erases
everything before it. ("That's a nice haircut but . . ."; "I
think your new boyfriend is great but . . .") *"But I know* that
even now God will give you whatever you ask," Martha
said. "I believe that you are the Christ, the Son of God."

There's Martha. Her eyes are swollen, her heart is
fractured, and the sound of wailing echoes from the walls
of her home yet she still believes there's more to her circumstances than just grief and moaning and the prevailing
stench of death. We stand alongside her in our own way—
the limping throng who have been beaten down, wearied
by trials, bruised from the past, and flogged by circumstances but in the end we cling to the smallest shred of

faith. *I know I lost my job but . . . I know he left me for another woman but . . . I know my son is on the streets but . . . I know my spouse is dead but . . . I know my mother's an alcoholic but . . . I know my dream has shattered but . . . I know I can't have children but . . . I know my brother Lazarus has died but . . . I—still—believe.* I scribbled down a quote from French philosopher and scientist René Descartes below my notes about Martha in my notebook. "He who gives the grace to believe other things can also give us grace to believe that He exists." Even in grief Martha's belief was swelling.

I read through the story again and contemplated Martha's faith, which I imagine volleyed from trust to confusion then to doubt and anger during her brother's illness and eventual death. I wondered if all of those feelings weren't elements of faith? In my head I could hear The Boyfriend's mother from college saying, "You need to work at getting more faith, Donna!" Doesn't faith require a *degree* of confusion, doubt, and questions? After Mother Teresa died many of her personal letters surfaced reflecting her own doubts and crises of faith. Journalists skewered her, calling her tormented, miserable, and troubled. But as Mother Teresa cradled death and misery every day on her lap in the streets of Calcutta it's amazing to me that she didn't doubt or question God *more*. If faith came with a guarantee, some sort of spiritual warranty, then we'd never have an opportunity for it. God could just drop it in a bag and hand it to us like some eternally happy retail clerk. Unlike The Boyfriend's mother, Martha (like Mother Teresa) didn't wear her faith like a silk scarf draped around her neck. She gripped it between her hands like a worn cotton rag stained with the blood, sweat, and tears of her life's trials. I jotted down in my notebook that like Harriet Beecher Stowe said, the All Wise had thought beyond the words of Martha's prayers and had given her the real thing.

I don't remember much about these days that I turned time and again to this story. It wasn't a remarkable week; I imagine it was ordinary in every way, right down to the weather and what I ate for lunch but somewhere in the mundane I realized that broken dreams are the launch pad to growth. The person who emerges from the pain is either stronger for it or strangled by it. For years I had focused on myself: What's wrong with my body? Why can't they fix my problem? What am I supposed to do? Why did I go into Kevin Taylor's bedroom? The problem with unful-filled dreams is that they give us tunnel vision; we focus on ourselves, and that can be a depressing and discouraging place to look. Self-absorption is abusive, unforgiving, critical, intolerable, disappointed, angry, shameful, and always impatient. We look to ourselves for the answers and become frustrated and despondent when we don't have them. TV and magazine covers shout, "Take a look at yourself! You suck and need to do something about it." What's ironic is that God calls us to examine ourselves only two times in the Bible (in I Corinthians 11:28, it says we should examine ourselves before taking communion and in II Corinthians 13:5, we are asked to examine whether we are in the faith, not just drifting along and sampling the new thing on the market but genuinely grounded in the truth of God's Son). Neither of these instances has anything to do with our looks, job, status, power, or family but we continue to spin our wheels and to juggle plates in an effort to whittle down our life to something we can manage.

At some point we throw up our hands but then what? It seems that we either continue to fight and wrestle, or we relinquish the plan as *we've* always known it in order to discover The Creator's dream for our life. When we admit our helplessness in driving our own dream and acknowledge God's divine power and goodness, we open the door to grace. Supreme Court justice Oliver Wendell Holmes, Jr., said, "The great act of faith is when man decides that he is not God." On an unremarkable, common day in the year 2000, my hands were shaking and my heart was sore as I let go of the wheel of the plan that I had been driving and took that act of faith.

◆ ◆ ◆

E I G H T

All life is a series of accidents but when you find most of
them pointing all one way, you may guess that there is
something behind them that is not an accident.

—GEORGE BERNARD SHAW, PLAYWRIGHT

AND AUTHOR

THE FERTILITY SPECIALIST RECOMMENDED WE try intrauterine insemination (IUI), which is what our former
specialist suggested before I contracted the virus in Missouri. I'd give myself shots in the leg, at the end of those
rounds Troy would give me a shot in my hip muscle, then a
nurse would insert a catheter into my uterus for a "deposit."
It sounded perfectly unpleasant in every way and Troy was
nervous about giving me a shot. We'd had friends who had
also gone through the same process and the husband had
passed out in the middle of giving his wife the shot. I

thanked our friends for telling us that story and picked Troy up off the floor. "You can do it," I said.

"No, I can't. I can't stick a needle into someone."

"It won't be a problem."

"It is a problem," he said. "I know I can't do it."

"Listen! I have been poked, prodded, and probed in every way. You are *going* to do this." A few days later we shuffled off to the fertility clinic so Troy could learn how.

I had a sinus infection and was feverish on the day of our appointment. We opened the door to the clinic and every seat was taken in the waiting room. "Wow! Is this the lottery?" Troy asked. A wave of heat hit me in the face and I felt my head swim.

"Why is it so *hot* in here?" I asked. I asked that *several* times that morning. We found a spot against the wall and stood there till a couple of seats opened up. Throughout our wait Troy voiced his concern about passing out while giving me the shot. "You'll be fine," I said. It became increasingly aggravating. *I'll pass out.* "You'll be fine." *I'll pass out.* "You'll be fine." After a long, sweaty wait a short, dark-haired nurse led us to a small room where it was hot enough to bake cookies.

"We're having a problem with our heating system today," she said. With my sinuses blocked I could feel the blood vessels in my head swell in the heat. The nurse popped in a video for us to watch that featured a happy, infertile couple. They were all atwitter with infertility. The wife had bright red lips and long blood-red fingernails that clicked when she tapped the needle, preparing it for injection. I couldn't imagine ever being so well manicured for a shot. When the doctor initially explained the shots to me, he said I could give myself shots in the thigh or stomach. The thought of giving myself a shot in the stomach is equivalent to driving over a bridge so I chose the leg. When the needle was prepped the woman lifted her teal green sweater and plunged it into her abdomen. My stomach flip-flopped and Troy screamed. He says he didn't but even with a fever I remember hearing a scream that was not my own. The man stepped forward and then prepared his needle. He was handsome and brave and empathetic as he plunged the needle into the hip of his smiling wife. There. It was done. Perhaps to end the video they kissed or held each other in a loving embrace; I don't recall. My stomach was churning and I was anxious to leave the tiny sweatbox.

My legs felt like Jell-O as I followed the nurse to yet another small room. The good news in that room was that the heating problem *still* existed and my nausea was increasing!

"Has the doctor explained that these medicines will increase your chances of getting pregnant," the nurse said, "but that there are still no guarantees?" There was that annoying word *but* again that erases everything before it. My heart sank. I was so tired of these clinics and their pep talks. The nurse picked up an orange and showed Troy how to insert a needle into it. He did it a couple of times and then nodded as if to say he was a pro now. Moving on, the nurse had me lean forward onto a table as she filled a needle with saline solution. She put up her index and middle finger to form the peace sign. "Now Troy," she said, placing her fingers on my upper hip, "make sure you give the shot right in the middle of your two fingers here because if you give it over here to the right you could hit her sciatic nerve and paralyze her." My stomach stopped flopping and dropped out altogether.

Troy plunged the needle into my hip and I could feel the cold saline solution travel all the way down my leg and into my toes. It felt like all the blood in my head was in a race to get to my feet and as I leaned up I said, "I'm not feeling so . . ." I was about to fall spread eagle on the floor when the nurse caught me and helped me to a chair. She put my head between my knees, which is both ladylike and humiliating, and then left the room for a cold cloth. Thankfully, she left the door open so everyone from the office could see me as they walked by.

An astute nurse stuck her head inside the door and said, "Did you just pass out?"

"No, no," I said, waving my hand above me. "I just like to sit like this." I turned my head to see Troy standing at my side still holding the needle.

He smiled and leaned down to me. "I'm so happy I didn't pass out," he said. I didn't have the strength to smack him.

The nurse returned with a cold cloth and a cup of water. She sat across from us with a lap full of small bottles and needles. "This is what you'll be getting," she said, lifting a small bottle of medicine in front of us. "Insert the needle in here, fill it up, then give yourself the shot once a day." Then in a strange, surreal moment she belched. Sometimes a hiccup or a cough can be mistaken for a gastrointestinal moment but there was no mistaking this for what it was. She didn't say excuse me, she didn't even cock her head or lift her eyebrows in recognition of it; she just belched and then barreled on. "Use up all the vials," she said, continuing her instruction. She looked down at her lap and then to the chairs beside her. "Hold on. I forgot something." She jumped up and left the room.

Troy waited a moment and then whispered, "Did she just belch?" I started to laugh and nodded. "That wasn't a burp. That was a *belch*, right?"

"She didn't even say excuse me," I said, laughing. "Or, *whoa where'd that come from?*"

We stifled ourselves when she came back holding another vial. "This is what your vial will look like, Troy." We both stared at the vial and nodded with great interest. "Just do exactly what you did here today." Then . . . she belched again. I looked down at my washcloth and twisted it in my hands to keep from looking at her or Troy. She talked for a couple of minutes and then excused herself again.

"What is going on?" Troy said, whispering. He spun in his chair and looked around. "Are there cameras in this room? Is this some sort of experiment?" We both laughed till we cried. Given our chances, it seemed like the only thing to do.

I AUDITIONED FOR AND GOT a role in an ensemble play at a local professional theater. The play was written by an up-and-coming playwright from out of state and since the play was set in the South, Nashville was chosen as the debut of this new work. There were four women in the play and three of them were filled with too much angst for me. When I auditioned I only read for the role of the comedic woman and got the part.

One of the clients I had worked for several years ago called me out of the blue one day and said, "I heard you were back in town. I have a couple of huge projects coming up. Would you be interested in the work?" That work kept me scrambling during the day and then I went to rehearsals in the evenings. One of the actresses was a bold, outspoken woman who had an opinion for everything from politics to baking soda. One evening as she pulled her hair back to prepare for her part she said, "What the hell is the deal with all those WWJD bracelets that people wear? What's that mean again?"

"What would Jesus do," one of the actors said.

"Those damn bracelets drive me crazy. How the hell would I know what Jesus would do?" she said. "I mean, he *was* the son of God! He was perfect. The people he hung out with were perfect."

"No, they weren't," I said.

She looked at me in the mirror. "What?"

"Those people weren't perfect."

"They weren't?"

"No. They were just run-of-the-mill people."

I don't remember the rest of our conversation but her

comments stayed with me for days. "I'm going to write a book," I said to Troy.

"Does it start with, 'It was raining real hard the day we buried my daddy'"? he asked, remembering what I told him years ago.

It didn't; at least not this one. I wanted to take the stories of the apostles, the men who were with Christ daily, and give them texture and sound and smell. I wrote that book between writing assignments and Troy sent the first few chapters to a small publishing house. To my surprise they wanted to see the rest of the book and followed up with an offer. Without noticing, I had become a full-time writer.

THE FIRST IUI DIDN'T WORK. I was now a pro at disappointment. Several friends along the way all offered the same advice at this time. "You know, you can always adopt." Actually, I heard this a lot.

My internal rumblings were always the same: "*Really?* Thank you so much. I *never* knew that."

And there were always the few who would regale me with stories of someone they knew who was infertile but *then* they started the process for adoption and got pregnant. "Maybe you should start adoption papers and see if you get pregnant." No matter what you're going through you can be assured of advice from stupid people. Even though I had internally released the plan I was driving, it still hurt when medical news was always the same. But now it was different. I had the sense that something was up; I had no idea what or even what it meant but for the first time in my life there was this indescribable feeling that all of this was going somewhere.

One afternoon I went into Nashville to pick up our next round of shots from the pharmacy and on my way home I stopped at the grocery store. I was standing at the checkout when I noticed a man in the line next to me. A small Asian girl was in the front of his grocery cart and he was playing with her. She shrieked when he crept his fingers up her leg and then tickled her belly. He did it over and over, and each time she giggled from the end of her toes. As he paid and prepared to leave I watched as the toddler reached her arms for him and he lifted her out of the cart. She smushed his face between her tiny hands and then wrapped her arms around his neck. *She doesn't know,* I thought. *She doesn't know he doesn't look like her.* That visual image of the little girl's arms around her father stayed with me long after I had unpacked my groceries.

* * *

▓ AFTER WORKING ONE AFTERNOON I opened the Gospel of John. I read about a man who had been born blind. All his neighbors and the townspeople referred to him as Blind Guy. One day Christ saw him and restored the man's sight. With new eyes, ones that were no longer cloudy and unfocused, Blind Guy's neighbors didn't even recognize him. Some said, "Isn't this Blind Guy who used to sit and beg?" Others said, "No, that's not Blind Guy. He only looks like Blind Guy."

"It *is* me," the man formerly known as Blind Guy said. He told them that Jesus touched his eyes, giving him sight for the first time in his life.

The religious leaders were outraged, saying Christ couldn't be from God because he worked on the Sabbath. Around and around they went, bickering among themselves about this travesty. Finally, they sent for the man's parents and asked if he was really their son, the blind kid who had grown up to become Blind Guy. They affirmed he was. The religious leaders sent for the man formerly known as Blind Guy *again.* "The man who made you see is a sinner," they said, pointing their righteous fingers in his face.

He shrugged. "Could be," he said. "I don't know. All I

know is that I never saw one thing a day in my life and now I do."

"Well, how'd he do it?" they asked. "What'd he do to you?"

"I already *told* you. Why do you keep asking me? Do you want to become his disciples, too?"

The religious leaders began to hurl insults at him. For years they had ignored Blind Guy, so much so that when he began walking around the town they didn't even *recognize* him. Now seeing, Blind Guy had had enough. "Nobody has ever heard of opening the eyes of a man born blind," he said, looking them straight in the eyes. "If this man weren't from God he could do nothing." Then, not sharing in Blind Guy's happiness over his new sight, the religious leaders picked him up by the scruff of the neck and threw him out of their presence.

The text says that Christ heard about what happened and found the man formerly known as Blind Guy. He *found* him, which implies that he went out looking for him. In the early 1950s, Ralph Ellison wrote *Invisible Man*, a book about life as an African American in a white society. "I am an invisible man," he said. "I am a man of substance, of flesh and bone, fiber and liquids—and I might even be said to possess a mind. I am invisible, understand, simply because people refuse to see me." For centuries, society has had a way of ignoring, demeaning, and rejecting people they don't want to see. People had refused to see Blind Guy but The Christ not only looked for him but found him.

Augustine, the fourth-century Latin philosopher and scholar, spent much of his life studying the world's philosophies and said that in them he discovered that *man is looking for God*. When he was in his thirties Augustine opened the Gospel of John and his life was transformed when he read verse fourteen of chapter one: *The Word became flesh and made his dwelling among us. We have seen his glory, the glory of the One and Only, who came from the Father, full of grace and truth.* "In John 1:14," Augustine said, "I find that God is looking for man!" In God's pursuit of the human soul, English poet Francis Thompson referred to him as the Hound of Heaven, "those strong Feet that followed, followed after." In Thompson's case the Hound of Heaven found him wandering as an opium-addicted street vagrant. The Hound of Heaven continues to find people in boardrooms, chatrooms, and hospital rooms; on streetcars, ferries, and airplanes; in locker rooms, race cars, and football fields; at the bottom of a bottle, at the end of a line of cocaine, or the other side of a roulette wheel; on a dark street turning tricks or in a penthouse

turning tricks; on movie sets, fishing boats, and fashion run-
ways; in theaters, museums, and peep shows. He finds us
every millisecond of every second of every minute of the
day.

I scrambled for my notebook one day and wrote below
the story of Blind Guy something German poet and novelist
Rainer Maria Rilke said. "First you must find God somewhere, experience Him as infinitely, prodigiously, stupen-
dously present, then whether it be fear, or astonishment, or
breathlessness, whether it be, in the end, love with which
you comprehend Him, it hardly matters at all." I had always
known God but for the first time in my life I felt like I was
actually finding him.

In the disappointment and frustration of infertility I
was beginning to comprehend a God that shattered my
childish perceptions. I sensed that I hadn't been forgotten
or unseen in Kevin Taylor's bedroom. For years I had
asked, even demanded to know, where God was that day
and now I knew. He was there, *distressed in my distress*, pursu-
ing not only mine but a molester's soul as well.

N I N E

Great is the God who makes us wise. And how does He
make us wise? By that very grief which we flee and from
which we seek to hide ourselves.

—NIKOLAI VASILIEVICH GOGOL, RUSSIAN AUTHOR

AND DRAMATIST

THE SECOND ROUND OF IUI didn't work. Our doctor recommended one more round but if that didn't work we
should then consider in vitro fertilization (IVF). He explained that we had a 50/50 chance with IVF but the ex-
penses were far greater than IUI. I had long suffered with
migraine headaches and in the previous weeks they had
gotten worse. I couldn't sleep well at night and felt terrible
when I woke up each morning. It felt as if all of my physical
problems magnified after my last appointment with the

fertility specialist so I made an appointment to see our family physician.

Throughout his examination he questioned me about my symptoms and followed up with further questions about what was happening in my life. He leaned against the computer stand in the exam room and looked at me. "You're suffering from depression."

That didn't sound right. I had never struggled with melancholy feelings; I was generally a happy, content person. I didn't even *feel* depressed. "I don't feel depressed at all," I said. "I'm still doing my work. I'm still doing everything the same, really."

"Your situation is an emotional one," he said. "Even if you don't think it is, your body knows it is." He sounded like the physician in Missouri. "I don't want to medicate you." (How startling to hear this in the country that leads the world in antidepressant prescriptions.) "Don't try to cover up your sadness. Admit it but don't medicate it. Exercise. Cut out junk food, eat well, and get good rest at night. You'll make it through." It was possibly the best prescription a doctor ever gave me.

Our culture views pain as something that should at least be minimized if not obliterated altogether. We admit we feel bad but we want *instant* elimination of any traces of suffering. We tend to live in a happiness-centered society and if we're not truly happy then something must be terribly wrong and off-balance. We like to reduce life down to something we can manage and feel God should not only defer to our plan but fully cooperate with it. But when he doesn't and our plan goes awry we're insistent that someone or *something* ease our heartache immediately. We use or abuse anything or anyone to help us survive life, feeling it's the best we can do. We arrange our lives to alleviate disappointment, frustration, dissatisfaction, and pain, viewing them as enemies of our soul. But are they *always* bad? Can't disappointment and broken dreams actually be good if we listen to what our life is saying through them? If we allow them, if we can stand the pull, broken dreams *can* lead to higher dreams. I didn't know it then but I was on my way to that higher dream.

I HAD FINISHED THE BOOK I was writing and turned it in to the publisher. Troy was working with Eddie Carswell and NewSong on their new album and Eddie had read a poem by Samuel Taylor Coleridge that likened friendship to a sheltering tree. Eddie had written a song around that concept and Troy suggested that the group release a gift book at the same time as the album, revolving around friendship. "You could write it," he said to me one evening. "Maybe you could interview people about a significant friendship in their lives." It sounded interesting and Troy put together a proposal and asked the same publishing house that was releasing my first book if they'd be interested. They were, so I got busy. As I began shots for our third round of IUI, it dawned on me one day between the writing work I was getting on the side and writing for the new book that I might actually be able to make a living as a writer.

I WENT WITH MY FRIEND Deb to a women's seminar one evening that covered everything from the perspective of a woman's health and wellness. We sat next to a longtime friend of Deb's who worked in another city as a therapist and family counselor. She was easy to talk to and had a tremendous sense of humor. One of the evening's speakers spoke about the effects of childhood sexual abuse and during the break that followed Deb and her friend continued the discussion in the vestibule. When Deb stepped away for a cup of coffee I kept the conversation alive with her therapist friend and shared what happened all those years ago. I felt safe with her because I didn't know her, she *was* a counselor, and she lived in another city. She pointed out that she noticed I had waited till Deb stepped away before I broached the topic. "It's such an awkward thing to talk about," I said, searching for words that made sense.

She asked if I had forgiven my molester. "Absolutely," I said.

"Was it easy to forgive?"

I thought about it. "I don't know. I think it was. I never really blamed him so I never thought he needed forgiveness."

"Why wouldn't you blame him? He violated you, not the other way around."

"Right. I know that."

"Do you? Really?" She leaned against the wall and looked at me. "Have you ever owned the pain of that day?"

That seemed like a stupid question. "Of course I own it," I said. "It happened to me."

"No," she said. "Have you ever acknowledged the pain? Have you ever said, 'What *he* did really hurt like hell?' There's a difference." I stood quietly, processing what she had said. "Forgiveness doesn't let him off the hook; it lets you off the hook."

The break was over and there wasn't time to talk but I thought about what she had said for days after that. For years I had denied the pain and emotions, and continued to stuff it down and suck it up. I had always taken the pain of that day and acknowledged it as repercussions of my own actions; I had brought on the pain because it was my fault. Business as usual, you know. It seems we're all good at that. But if we continue to deny the hurt, the pain, and the suffering, or shove it down or mask it with drugs, alcohol, sex, or work I wonder if we deny ourselves the grace of God? For the first time in years I began to doubt my thirty-plus years of self-made reasoning.

A COUPLE OF WEEKS LATER I turned the TV on late one evening and a station was about to air the *Leave It to Beaver* pilot episode from April 1957. I had only watched *Leave It to Beaver* a handful of times in my life but thought the pilot episode might be interesting because I'm always intrigued with the genesis of any project. I watched and discovered that Beaver's father, Ward, and his brother, Wally, were portrayed by different actors from the ones in the long-running series. In it, Beaver and his big brother, Wally, mistakenly receive a bicycle from a popular television show's contest. An executive from the show discovers the error and comes to the boys' house to claim the bicycle. Oh, the disappointment! Ward, the boy's suit-wearing and sagelike father, dispensed all the wisdom he could in the allotted twenty seconds remaining in the scene. He said, "A responsible person doesn't take things he hasn't earned. You have to be worthy of what you get in life. You have to work for it." For some strange reason these words bounced in my head. I know that the boys' father was talking about work and honesty and character but nearly every word rang out as the antithesis of grace. From the hand of Providence, a person *does* take what he *hasn't* earned. He does *not* have to be *worthy*, and he does *not* have to work for it. He doesn't have to keep doing, keep doing because it's already been done for him. Like any good introvert, I let that little twenty-second scene stew for days as I thought about it.

I STOPPED AT TROY'S OFFICE one afternoon so we could go to lunch together and as I was driving home I turned down the wrong street. I headed the other direction to get to the road I needed and stopped at a red light. Outside my driver's window was a schoolyard filled with children. I watched as a little five- or six-year-old girl dressed in pink began to jump. It was a clear day, perfect for jumping, but there was no reason to jump. No one had goosed her from behind, there was nothing to jump over; she wasn't even on a pogo stick. She just began to jump—hop, hop, hopping for no other reason than joy welling up inside of her, and she just couldn't contain herself. Her joy was so contagious that the little girl who had been playing with her also started to jump and together they bounced up and down, up and down. They jumped right in front of a teacher who sat in a lawn chair swinging her whistle around her finger and I noticed she never acknowledged the fantastic hopping that was taking place just a foot away from her.

The light turned green and I drove away thinking about those little girls. They loved hopping, playing, and just being part of life's landscape. I thought, *What if the little girl in pink went to a neighbor's house today and the man of the house or his son molested her? With all the innocence and joy just bouncing inside her, how could she ever see that evil act as her doing?* God communicates in surprising ways. He doesn't boom into our ears or send an angelic messenger. The fact is we couldn't handle either method. Angels are never depicted as sweet little cartoons in the Bible but as heavenly bodies whose appearance left people trembling on the floor, scared out of their wits. Imagine the pileup on the interstate if angels appeared in the passenger seat of even a handful of vehicles. The Creator speaks to us in unexpected ways, in out-of-the-way places and through unanticipated hopping. Sometimes, depending on the circumstances, his message can be easy to miss. I'm uncertain how many times he had tried to whisper words of my innocence to me in the previous years but driving down West End Avenue I finally heard them. My eyes filled and I let tears fall onto my lap. "It was your fault," I said aloud to Kevin Taylor, wherever he was in the world. "It was your fault, not mine. You did it. You hurt me. But I forgive you. Not because you've asked for it or would even care but because I don't want to be in bondage to you." I wiped my face with the palm of my hand and took my exit home. God won't fix the past but if we're willing, he can release us from it.

THE THIRD ROUND OF IUI failed but in a way I felt like I was being prepared for that. One afternoon I scribbled in my notebook: *Truth is, we don't like pain or grief or suffering of any kind. Humans prefer to avoid it altogether but God uses it for good. No pain, no growth. No suffering, no empathy. No grief, no compassion.* I read somewhere that Albert Einstein said, "It's not that I'm that smart; I just stay with problems longer," and added that to my notebook. It took me years of staying with my problems, most of them spent in the desert of Missouri, to realize that it wasn't all about me and my hang-ups or dreams. There was and will always be a higher dream. I was learning one of the mysteries of life.

I was reading the writings of the Psalms one morning

when I came across a verse I'm sure I'd seen before but it popped off the page as if new to this centuries-old book. In the 113th chapter I read that God "settles the barren woman in her home as the happy mother of children." I looked at the verse again, wondering if I'd read it correctly. There it was: "He settles the barren woman in her home as the happy mother of children." I turned the book upside down and inside out, looking for the word *biological* because I knew it had to be there. But it wasn't. It said the barren woman would be the happy mother of children. Period. It had been more than six years since I miscarried and in those years a lot of moments—key, life-changing moments—had accumulated, leading up to these words. In the living room of our condo I knew—not just felt, but *knew*—that Troy and I were supposed to be adoptive parents, just like Joseph and Mary who raised God's son as their own. Not bad company to be in. From that instance on I never viewed adoption as our Plan B or a last-ditch effort to have children. I never saw it as second rate or that I was somehow less of a woman because I couldn't carry children. I saw it then as I see it today . . . as my destiny of grace. I have no doubts about it.

"I don't think we're supposed to even try IVF," I told Troy that afternoon. "I think we're supposed to adopt."

He pumped his hand in the air. "That's what I've been saying all along," he said. He leaned against the kitchen counter. "Should we look here in the states or overseas?"

"China comes to mind," I said. I didn't know why. I hadn't known anyone who had adopted from China.

"That's what I've been thinking, too," Troy said.

We couldn't explain why we both thought of China. Perhaps we'd seen a news story about foreign adoptions and it featured Chinese children, or maybe we'd seen a flyer somewhere along our journey and the images of Asian faces had stayed with us, or maybe it's that we were both discerning the Whisper in our soul. I was no longer struggling against God and his "inept" plan but receiving an eternal embrace. Our pastor shared something in his message one Sunday morning from Martin Luther, and I scrambled as fast as I could to write it down. "Oh!" Luther said. "His grace and goodness towards us is so immeasurably great, that without great assaults and trials it cannot be understood." For the first time in my life I *did* understand.

IF WE DON'T GIVE OURSELVES over to bitterness, a fresh wisdom comes alive in those who are on the backside of broken dreams. It's a calm, yet vibrant wisdom that helps us discover new and higher dreams. It comes with a fresh discernment of who and what we need to leave behind, reminding us that there is a big difference in remembering guilt and carrying guilt. We know that we have been slow, even negligent, in offering grace to ourselves and understand that it will take time to rebuild what we took years to destroy.

This fresh wisdom tells us what our limitations and strengths are and for the first time in our lives, we're okay with that. We've come to terms with the fact that we'll always be a work in progress. We are ushered into a way of life we've never experienced before because we look at the pain from our past and those who caused it, and for once we don't think about those people with anger. In our innermost self we forgive them because we understand that unforgiveness ultimately destroys us, not them. We realize that those who have wronged us are as broken as we are and if our journey's been rough we can only imagine what it's been like for them. This wisdom invites us to uncover the wounds we've kept wrapped for a lifetime and let the All Wise improve us in that unwrapping. It helps us see our stumblings and failures as a vital part of the journey and that we wouldn't be who we are today without them and we realize there will be plenty more on the road ahead. We know we can no longer stay put but we must seize the day because we are called to a new beginning, a new dawn.

When we read the words of Jesus to a lame man, "Do you want to be well?" our broken hearts and crippled spirits cry, "Yes! Yes! Yes!" And even though it's so much easier to keep dragging our baggage with us we work on getting rid of it, piece by painful piece. We know that we have lived and will continue to live a flawed and imperfect life but we also understand that the light of God can only get in through our cracks. This wisdom awakens in our soul the realization that there is a *Divine* plan for us. There is a Divine *plan* for us. There is a Divine plan *for* us. There *is* a Divine plan for *us*. We no longer need to plead as a line from Mozart's Requiem begs, "Remember, merciful Jesu, that I am the cause of your journey," because we at last believe that he does not need the reminder. We *are* the cause of his journey. *We* are the cause of his journey. We are *the* cause of his journey. That knowledge buckles our knees and we tremble before God, asking, "Why me? Why choose or love me?" Life words finally move from our head to our heart and we *embrace the fact* that we are not only loved and accepted but *pursued* by God. We realize that *if* we believe there's something more we can do to earn that love, we snub our nose at God and his message of grace because we don't have to do *anything* but come. We don't have to *do* one thing. We no longer think of God as a casual acquaintance who shows up for major holidays and birthdays.

This wisdom humbles our heart and opens our eyes to the power, majesty, and holiness of God. It looks in the mirror and realizes that with each day that passes, time is running out and that realization magnifies in our souls what is most important in the days or years that are left. We discover, along with English poet Elizabeth Barrett Browning, that "God keeps his holy mysteries just on the outside of man's dream" but that many of them can be discovered. It is a wisdom that sees the stars, oceans, mountains, breath, a baby's smile, and hopping little girls as gifts. This new wisdom is a triumph of grace.

WE FOUND AN ADOPTION AGENCY and started the paperwork. We called our home states of Ohio and New York and requested our birth certificates and marriage license. Each document had to be stamped with the great seal of each state. We had our physicals, got our police clearance, had blood drawn, submitted the last five years of tax returns, got fingerprinted by the Tennessee Bureau of Investigation, described in detail many moments of our childhood, wrote pages and pages that equaled the length of a thesis of why we wanted to be parents and how we would do it, and got fingerprinted by the FBI. Most of this paperwork had to be notarized and then stamped with the "Great Seal of the State of Tennessee." At one point I clarified to our social worker that she knew we were trying to adopt an infant, not break into the Pentagon.

At the beginning of our paperwork I had questioned many times how we would pay for all the fees associated with an adoption. I knew we didn't have extra money just sitting around. Many times I prayed, "How are we going to do this?" At every step I received more writing work. One of the big projects I worked on never materialized for the company who hired me and with the exception of a final paycheck, I was paid for every single word I wrote. By the time we turned our paperwork into China I had received more freelance work than I ever had and we paid every single bill. Now came the wait. Waiting for an adoption to finalize is like being pregnant but without the vomiting.

IN JULY 2000, TROY AND I drove to Knoxville to see NewSong in concert. It was a blazing hot day and as we stood backstage talking with Eddie Carswell he told me about a song he was thinking of writing. He didn't say much, just a couple of sentences. "A little boy's mother is sick around Christmastime," he said, "and he wants to buy her a pair of shoes so she'll look pretty when she gets to heaven." That's all he said. "Do you think that would make a good song?"

People have long offered me ideas for stories but whereas those suggestions have never registered with me, something fired in my head that day. "I actually think that would make a good book," I said.

"Then get to writing it," Eddie said. "You're the one with the computer."

In the weeks following I jotted down some plot points and character details and began to flesh out an outline. It takes much less time to write a four-minute song than a book so Eddie finished and had the song produced before I completed the novel. He called one evening and played it for Troy and me. We loved it.

"We need a name for it," Eddie said. "Do you think we should go with 'Christmas Shoes' or 'The Christmas Shoes'?"

"'The,'" I said.

"So will you title your book, *The Christmas Shoes*?" he asked.

I laughed. "If there *is* a book! Sure."

The song was released to radio in December 2000, and

in three weeks it shot to number one on the Billboard chart. *USA Today* and other papers ran an article about the group and the song, and a literary agent named Jennifer Gates saw the article and tracked down NewSong's management company in Nashville, which was Troy. Jen asked if anyone had considered writing a book called *The Christmas Shoes*. Troy grimaced at what he was about to say. For years someone would say to him, "You need to hear my wife sing. She's great!" But she wasn't. Or, "You *have* to hear my daughter. She sounds just like Mariah Carey." But she didn't. Troy said, "Well, actually, my wife is currently writing a book." He couldn't see her but imagined Jen groaning and rolling her eyes on the other end of the line.

The next day Jen called me. She said that she and one of the firm's partners, Esmond Harmsworth, would love to see my outline for the book. I imagined a weighty name like Esmond Harmsworth had to be attached to a man in his late fifties or early sixties with a full, gray beard, wearing tweed jackets and smoking a pipe. He was none of the above. My first perceptions have always stunk. No one had ever requested to see one of my outlines and I felt silly sending off my rambling thoughts and disjointed sentences. Jen telephoned a few days later and asked how quickly I could complete the manuscript. "When do you need it?" I asked.

"Oh, there's no hurry," she said. "Yesterday would be nice but there's really no rush." I finished it within two weeks and sent it to her.

We were preparing for a vacation in Alaska to celebrate my in-laws' wedding anniversary when Jen called and said the manuscript would be put up for auction among publishing houses in New York. I spoke with several editors on the phone about the book, including Jennifer Enderlin at St. Martin's Press and then three days later boarded the plane for Alaska. Jen called Troy's cell phone while we were in the Chicago O'Hare Airport for a layover. "Congratulations," she said. "St. Martin's Press picked up *The Christmas Shoes*." I called Eddie and shared the news with him; after all, he had inspired the idea on a hot, sweltering July day.

"Well, look at what God did," Eddie said.

Before the book was released to the public a movie producer in Los Angeles read the galley copy and decided she wanted to turn the book into a made-for-TV-movie. The book released in November 2001, and landed on the *New York Times* and the *USA Today* bestseller lists. I include these details and series of events not to merely rattle off the steps as they happened but to relay that none of that had been part of *my* plan or *my* childhood dream. Mine was a good, solid dream but it was only when it crumbled that I discovered the better, higher dream.

THE DAYS AND WEEKS TURNED into one month after another as we waited for word about travel. People constantly asked, "When will you leave for China?" and we always said the same thing: "We don't know." Many friends would say, "This is like the pregnant part of waiting for a baby." I've never known any woman who carried a baby for sixteen months! Week after week I complained to Troy, "In a country of over one billion people you'd think they'd have enough people to speed this process up a little!"

In February 2002, I was visiting relatives in east Tennessee doing research for what would become *The Angels of Morgan Hill* ("It was raining real hard the day we buried my daddy."). My aunts Geraldine and Maxine drove me around Greene County to meet with farmers who had raised tobacco all their lives and others who would help me bring to life rural Tennessee of the 1940s. I spoke with Troy a couple of times during my time there and drove the four hours home on Saturday afternoon. I walked into the

---

condo and talked with Troy about my trip before heading to the kitchen for a bite to eat.

When I turned the corner, balloons and streamers popped out at me from the kitchen and the sweetest little Asian face peered at me from huge pictures lining the countertop. She had enormous black eyes, wispy black hair, and little red lips that were formed in a perfect O. In a separate picture she was sitting in a baby walker with her foot propped up as if relaxing, and in the third photo a Chinese woman was holding her but the baby was peering anxiously into the camera lens. She was beautiful. Troy had received our referral the day before but never hinted about it, saving the surprise. "I didn't think you would *ever* come in here," he said. "I was dying, waiting for you to turn that corner."

The images in those photos took my breath and I whispered, "Is this her?"

"That's her," he said. "We travel in six weeks."

I tried to read through the information we had on her but my eyes couldn't focus. "What does it say?"

"A policeman found her on the street and took her to the orphanage." As people shuffled about, running full speed, and zipping through their day, angels hovered around a small bundle on a busy street in China and waited for Destiny.

Tears fell down my face as I stared at her picture. We had already named her.

Grace.

T E N

Whenever I think calmly over all I have been through,
I come to the conclusion that there is a Providence who
has specially cared for me.

—PYOTR TCHAIKOVSKY, COMPOSER

THOSE LAST FEW WEEKS LEADING to travel were long and
tedious. We went through our travel checklist several
times, and packed and repacked our suitcases (okay, Troy
repacked mine), making everything fit. In the last several
months I had been going to garage and yard sales and visiting thrift stores to find baby things for the baby. I had
been invited to speak at a women's conference and one of
the other presenters was pregnant. The other speakers on
the docket rallied around her and asked all the right questions, oohing and aahing over her glowing appearance.
Although many friends and associates knew that Troy and

I were adopting, I didn't have the pregnant belly as a reminder and it stung as few people oohed and aahed over my upcoming arrival.

Two and a half weeks before traveling I ran into Gwen Amorim, the wife of a friend for whom I'd done writing work. Gwen is an unpretentious woman who goes about loving God and loving people in a quiet and unassuming way. I hadn't seen her in years and had only spoken to her casually in the past but she had heard we were adopting. The next day her husband called and asked if anyone was giving me a baby shower. No one had, so a week before we traveled Gwen hosted a party to celebrate Gracie's arrival. Her gracious spirit and attention to our impending "birth" was a sweet act of kindness that took me by surprise, sneaking in from the side—as grace always does.

WE DECIDED WE WANTED TO document our journey for Gracie so Troy purchased a small journal for our trip. Despite the few notebook entries you've read in this book it should be noted that I'm not a journaler by nature. I do try to jot down an idea or a thought on a scrap piece of paper stuck to the bottom of my purse when I'm writing a book but half the time I can't read my own handwriting.

I'll pull out my notes when I begin to write and say, "What in the world does 'fishbeak' mean? Does that even say 'fishbeak'? I wonder where I was going with that."

I opened the journal and concentrated on writing legibly. I wrote an introduction to her and then on the second page I wrote, in part:

We loved you in our hearts long before we ever saw you because God had chosen you for us before any of us were even born. We are all the chosen ones. He had chosen us for you and you for us. It was all part of His design and plan. We are all adopted into God's family. It is our prayer that you will always know how much we love you. You are ours. It is our prayer that you will always know how much God loves you. You are His. He gave His son for you. He wants to have a relationship with you. You can talk to Him at any time and tell Him anything. He's big enough to handle it. He loves you. Don't ever forget that.

Half the battle in life is knowing what not to forget and forgetting what doesn't need to be remembered. We remember the bad stuff and forget the good. We let toxic memories seep into our souls and hearts to poison our day, while the good and holy memories are cast aside to be glanced at only on occasion. I prayed that Gracie would take more than the occasional glance.

On the night before we traveled my mother called from Ohio to get our final travel arrangements. Although my parents would be unable to drive to Nashville for Gracie's homecoming they wanted to know when we'd be back in the country with their first granddaughter. Before we hung up she said, "Grace will adjust fine. Children always know when they're loved."

We boarded the plane in Nashville on March 15, 2002, and flew past the sun into the night skies of China. We knew we would be landing in Beijing in the evening so we forced ourselves to stay awake, watching four of the five movies on the flight. When we landed we were numb from lack of sleep. We met Skip and Melissa Hagan, who were also adopting with our agency, and loaded into the van for the hotel. We'd meet the other families in the morning and spend two days sightseeing in Beijing before traveling to the Guangxi Province in south China for our girls.

Although all our travel suggestions had reminded us not to drink, taste, or even brush our teeth with the water in China, I had forgotten and brushed my teeth that evening as I would have at home. By the time I realized what I was doing it was too late but I thought, *I didn't drink it. Surely it won't be that bad.* It was all that and more. I ran for the bathroom sometime in the early morning hours and was fortunate enough to make several more related trips. "Guess they mean what they say about that whole water thing," Troy said, whispering in the darkness. I was too depleted to whack him.

We met the rest of the families in our group in the hotel lobby the next day. Dan and Janet Crowley lived in Chicago and had been married for several years without children. Tim and Laurie Richterkessing were from Minneapolis and were bringing home their first child. Kim Edwards had grown children but was childless with his second wife Jodi; they would take their little one back to Michigan to meet her older siblings. Skip and Melissa Hagan brought along their two biological daughters to meet their new sister. Jill Barker, Janet Ratzloff, and another single woman were all taking their babies home to families in Georgia, Michigan, and New York. A family from Mississippi was with us who also brought along their biological daughter, and we'd meet John and Pat Siefker and Jeff and Kristen Gowman two days later when we arrived in our girls' province. There were twenty-two of us, a diverse group from all parts of the United States but we had one common goal: We wanted to bring home our babies.

Time ticked slowly in Beijing. It was interesting to see Tiananmen Square, the Forbidden City, and the Great Wall, but there was one prevailing thought in all of our minds: We wanted to bring home our babies! On the evening of March 17, we watched an acrobatic show filled with lots of young children. Our translator, Joy, a young woman in her early twenties, informed us that the children had all lived in orphanages but now traveled with the show. I couldn't watch in the same way after that—knowing that the children on stage didn't have families to love and care for them but would spend their lives traveling in an acrobatic show.

The next morning Troy and I had breakfast in the hotel. As we left the restaurant I saw a Chinese baby with her adoptive parents. I stopped to talk with them and the baby raised her arms to hide her face. "She's shy," I said.

The mother shook her head. "No. She's been abused. She brings her arms up to protect herself." My heart sank at the horrific thought of a baby trying to protect herself.

Before we left Beijing Joy spoke into the microphone on the bus and said, "Thank you for coming to China to adopt the children and take them to America where they will have clean water, a good education, and a good home with a mommy and daddy who will take care of them. They are lucky babies." My eyes filled at her words and I noticed Melissa Hagan and Laurie Richterkessing both wiping tears from their faces. I didn't know much about the people in our group but I felt that none of their China dolls would ever have to raise their little arms to protect themselves against them.

We were scheduled to board a plane out of Beijing around 4 P.M. on March 18. Once we landed in Nanning we'd check into our hotel room and the orphanage would bring the babies to our rooms at 7 P.M. We arrived at the airport early and noticed that there wasn't a plane in sight as the time neared for our flight. Our translator checked on the plane several times and was told the same thing with each trip to the podium: "It will be here shortly." The four o'clock hour passed and we all grew restless. Didn't they understand that we wanted our babies? Another half hour passed with no sight of the plane. "It will be here shortly," the airline gatekeeper said. Troy took a nap and I flipped through every Chinese paper in the airport, wondering what the headlines said. The second hour of our wait arrived and I was ready to hurt someone but maintained a seething measure of grace. As the third hour approached I saw a plane landing on the runway.

"Let's hope and pray that's our plane," Troy said.

We boarded and were still being seated when the plane began to taxi down the runway. The carry-on bins above us were still open and Troy said, "Watch your heads," as he dove into his seat. There were no reminders to stow our items below our seats or in the carry-on bins, to buckle up, or to put our seat in the full and upright position. We just taxied and took off; the rest were minor details. I picked over the fish and rice that was served on the plane and passed on the dry-squid snack. I looked at my watch: It was 7:30 and we should have already had our babies.

It was after eight o'clock when we arrived at the airport in Nanning and a little after nine o'clock when we arrived at the hotel. The staff was gracious and warm as they checked us into our rooms but those few minutes in line felt like hours. As I stood in line with Troy I noticed a cargo van pull in front of the hotel. *Gracie could be in there,* I thought. I watched as a Chinese woman opened the side door and stepped out of the van holding a small child in her arms. She reached for another child and I could feel my heart race as another woman stepped out of the van holding a small bundle. "The babies!" I said, grabbing Troy's arm. "It's the babies. The babies are here." Every woman in our group ran for the doors.

Our new translator Shiyan waved her hands in the air. "Don't rush the babies," she said. "Please let them come into the hotel and we will deliver your daughter to your room as soon as you are checked in." We stopped and watched as a parade of Chinese women carried eleven little China dolls past us. Most of the babies were dressed in matching clothes of a yellow print sweatshirt and sweatpants.

"Where's Gracie?" I asked, looking into the face of each baby. The women were moving too fast.

"I can't tell which one she is," Troy said, holding the video camera. The last woman scurried past us but we couldn't identify Gracie. She had been seven months old in the pictures we'd received and now she was ten-and-a-half months. We received the key to our room and had just enough time to open the suitcase and locate the bottles, formula, diapers, and pajamas before we heard a commotion in the hallway. The porters were delivering luggage to each room as the babies were arriving!

We heard someone yell, "The babies are here!" The hall was filled with luggage racks, anxious parents, and women from the orphanage holding our children.

"Siefker," we heard Shiyan yell at the end of the hall.

"Right here," John said as he and Pat raised their hands above the sea of bodies. A sweet Chinese woman handed Emma over to her parents.

Shiyan looked through the papers in her hands. "Edwards," she yelled.

Kim and Jodi waved, and Shiyan brought Emily to her mom and dad. Troy and I stood on our toes trying to see them. "Crowley," Shiyan said above the noise.

Dan and Janet's door was open but they weren't in the hallway. "They're down here," Troy yelled from our end of the hall. We watched as a Chinese woman walked into the Crowleys' room. A baby girl who was sucking on her ring and middle fingers stared at her new parents. Janet reached out and touched her hand, letting Julia warm up to her.

The porters continued to deliver luggage while the babies began to cry. The hall buzzed with excitement and fear as one by one Shiyan united the babies with their parents. "Richterkessing," she said, looking at her papers.

"Right here," Tim said and the second baby named Emma was handed over to her mama.

"VanLiere," Shiyan shouted. From the time we had begun the paperwork we had waited twenty-two months—longer than the gestation of an elephant—for this moment.

"Down here," Troy said.

A Chinese woman smiled as she walked down the hall carrying the most beautiful baby we'd ever seen. Gracie's sweatshirt was tucked into her sweatpants and she looked like a tiny Sumo wrestler. I took Gracie from the woman and said, "We've been waiting for you!" Her black eyes were huge but expressionless as she stared at us. I imagined we were the whitest people she'd ever seen. I laughed and bounced her up and down. Troy held on to her hand and continued to videotape. She smelled like she'd just had a bath and her hair was firm from gel or hairspray.

Skip and Melissa received Janie next and Melissa laughed as her hand landed on Janie's bare bottom. She was wearing baby split pants that are common in China. (Just like the name implies, there's a split right in the back of a baby's pants providing easier access to the toilet without a diaper!) We moved closer to the Hagans so we could see Janie. Gracie never took her eyes off of me.

Shiyan explained that she would come by each of our rooms to fill out some paperwork and within seconds the hallway that had just been bustling with life was quiet as we all closed the door to our rooms behind us. I lay Gracie on the bed so we could count her fingers and toes while I changed her diaper. She lay motionless, staring at us, her dark little eyes moving from me to Troy and then to me again. I took off her sweatshirt and then her pants and Troy said, "What is that?" Her diaper was a rag that was held on by a bungee cord. I unhooked the bungee cord and took the wet rag off and she crossed her legs at the ankles. We laughed and uncrossed them only to have her cross them again. She let out a small cry, not one of distress but more like, "What's going on here?" and her voice was hoarse; she sounded like a little frog trying to croak. From the sound of it, I questioned if she had been crying for most of the day. Since she was wearing a rag I wondered if the common routine of lying down for a diaper was foreign to her. It became a game for us to uncross her ankles but Troy and I were the only ones laughing. I finally got a clean diaper on her and threw away the rag and bungee cord. She crossed her ankles again and lay scratching her belly. We laughed watching her and she continued to scratch, scratch, scratch, watching us. I pulled out a pair of pink pajamas and dressed her in them. I took pictures of Troy holding her and he took some of me with her. She's expressionless in each one. I held her close to me and felt in my bones that this was the better way that God had planned for not only Troy and me but for Grace as well. We were meant to be together.

Before we had left Nashville, Linda Prater, a longtime

friend had dropped by the condo one afternoon to bring a baby gift. She had adopted her daughter more than thirty years earlier. "No one can understand how special adoption is until they do it themselves," she said. "I can still remember the exact moment they placed my daughter in my arms. She looked right at me and I just *knew* she was mine. There was no doubt about it. And you'll know it, too." As I looked into Gracie's black eyes I knew it. I knew she was mine. She wasn't born through my body but in my heart—where grace is always birthed.

We tried giving her a bottle but she wouldn't have anything to do with it. If I even held it in front of her she would cry. She was not going to take a bottle from these foreign faces. Shiyan came to our room before eleven to go over paperwork and to take our first family picture together. "What is her middle name?" Shiyan asked.

"Zhenli," I said. I had worked with a Chinese woman in Nashville to help me find a Chinese word to help describe how we thought of Gracie. It means "priceless gift." Shiyan said the babies hadn't eaten and needed a bottle so after she left we tried feeding Gracie again. Her cries were louder and more hoarse with each attempt and it became frustrating and nerve-racking. In the end, she refused to take the bottle and we finally decided to put her to bed without dinner. We were well on our way to being parents of the year. We sang "Jesus Loves Me" to her and she stared into our faces, making us laugh. We lay her down at eleven o'clock and she didn't move or take her eyes off of us. We turned off the bedside light and waited for her to fall asleep. It dawned on me what I had done earlier in the evening and I crept to the bathroom and pulled the bungee cord out of the garbage, putting it in a bag with the clothes Gracie was wearing when she was handed to me. It was part of her journey to us, a reminder of where she had been. When we were assured that she was sleeping we got up and took pictures and videotape, watching her breathe. "She looks like a little angel, doesn't she?" Troy asked.

I nodded. "A little angel who sounds like a three-pack-a-day smoker." We both laughed and fought the urge to scoop her up. Many women in China approach adoptive parents and say, "Lucky baby. Lucky baby." I had heard it in the hall as some of the babies were being delivered and Troy and I talked about it as we watched Gracie sleep. To me, "lucky" has connotations of magic, sparkling leprechauns, a wink, and rolling dice. "Luck didn't have anything to do with it," I said, whispering to her. She was a gift. We had held out our arms for years; we had held them out till they ached and our bodies shook under the strain. Perhaps that is when a gift is most valued and loved. God is excessive, even reckless, when it comes to grace but it is never wasted and I wonder how often it is acknowledged. That night, Troy and I both recognized it and leaned down to kiss Gracie's face.

Shadowlands is the 1993 film that depicts the life of renowned author C. S. Lewis and his first and only marriage to Joy Davidman that took place when he was nearing sixty and Joy was battling cancer. She died four years after they married and Lewis's grief was profound. At the end of the movie, actor Anthony Hopkins, portraying Lewis, says, "Why love if losing hurts so much? I have no answers, only the life I have lived. Twice in that life I was given the choice, as a boy and as a man. The boy chose safety. The man chose suffering. The pain now is part of the happiness then. That's the deal." We can try to cover the pain, paint it a different color, or wish it away but in the end it's inevitable. It's part of the deal. We can't have one without the other.

Troy and I lay in the dark and listened to the small body next to us breathe in and out, in and out. Our happiness at that moment was part of the pain of childlessness. And I would have gone through it again for this night in Nanning.

E L E V E N

May the Almighty grant me just enough strength, before my end, to enable me to express in music the emotion which this undeserved act of spiritual grace has awakened in me.

—FRANZ JOSEPH HAYDN, COMPOSER

GRACIE FLEW THE THIRTEEN HOURS of flights like a pro and we arrived back in Nashville the day before Easter and were met at the airport by four friends and Troy's parents. As we walked toward them we could see Troy's mother crying, itching to get her hands on Gracie. "Here's Grandma," I said, handing Gracie to Vicki. Grace stared into each face and smiled. Like my mother told me before we left for China: Children always know when they're loved.

We drove to the condo and introduced Gracie to Bailey, who was now eleven years old. He looked at me as if saying, "I don't know what that is but feel free to take it back." In each picture Bailey is sitting at least a foot away from Gracie. His feelings never softened.

Gracie didn't like the idea of going to bed (her internal clock was still set for China hours and it was morning there) and she cried for four hours straight that evening. She cried three hours the next night, then two hours the next, and then finally slept through the night without a peep. She was an easy baby who loved to eat, sleep, and play, and fell into our routine as if she'd always been there. She laughed hard and played harder. She was so inquisitive and playful that she hated the thought of missing one second of fun and would stiffen when I picked her up and walked toward her bedroom. She just couldn't stand the idea of playtime being over for sleep! Books were her favorite toys so I'd read a couple of picture books to her before laying her down; then the crying would begin. On some days she'd cry for thirty minutes before falling asleep. I went to check on her one afternoon and found her clinging to the rails of the crib, her face smushed against them like a tiny prisoner. Once asleep she'd take long, three- to four-hour naps! When she awoke she liked to stay in her crib another thirty minutes or so to play and would cry if I tried to get her out before she was ready.

One afternoon my editor, Jennifer, called and asked if I'd thought of writing a follow-up to *The Christmas Shoes*. I hadn't. During Gracie's naps I was working on the novel I'd always wanted to write since college. Jen called several weeks later and asked if I'd thought any more about a follow-up. "Do *you* want me to write one?" I asked.

"We think it'd be a great idea," she said. In the days ahead I began to think of what a possible follow-up would look like: At the end of *The Christmas Shoes*, the young boy Nathan is now grown and is in medical school. Hmmm. . . . I barely passed science. How would I pull that off? Why didn't I say he was a journalism or English major? I sat down with a couple of doctors at Vanderbilt Hospital and called Skip Hagan (from our adoption group), who is an emergency room physician and they all agreed to help me with my research. I wrote much of it during Gracie's long three-to four-hour naps and took a couple of trips to my parents' house so they could spend time with her as I worked. Thinking of Gracie I titled the book, *The Christmas Blessing*, and dedicated it to her. She was a blessing of grace I never expected.

TROY AND I ALWAYS KNEW we wanted more children so in 2003, we began the paperwork for another adoption.

We went through all the rounds again: birth and marriage certificates, police and FBI clearance, fingerprints, blood tests, tax records, and wrote a paper called, "Why I Want to be a Parent . . . . Part II." We turned in all the notarized and state-sealed papers and waited to receive travel rights from Homeland Security (what used to be the Immigration and Naturalization Service). Our birth certificates were only good for six months and when Homeland Security had our paperwork for four months we were concerned. When they had it for five months we were really concerned. The adoption agency said we could call our local senator's office and ask that they make a call to Homeland Security. I called our local senator's office once, twice, then a third time and spoke to a very nice woman who was sympathetic to our situation. But I didn't want sympathy; I wanted action! During my fourth call to her I pointed out that we were trying to bring an infant into the country. Again, she said she was trying her best to move through the paperwork and was understanding of our circumstances but I felt she was powerless to do anything. As each day ticked away we became a bit anxious as we watched the mail. We had heard other stories of birth certificates lapsing while waiting for papers from Homeland Security and adoptive parents needing to go through the process again. The thought of starting over was becoming more real as each day passed and our aggravation and frustration with bureaucratic red tape was increasing. With a month left to spare, I went to the mailbox one afternoon and was relieved to *finally* pull out the paperwork we needed.

In June 2004, we received a referral for a little girl in China. Her eyes were big and round making her look more Spanish than Chinese. Her little mouth turned down in a slight frown and she looked so tiny in every picture. We had narrowed our list of names down to four but when we saw her sweet face we knew she was Kate, which means pure and virtuous, and that Meili was her middle name, which means "beautiful gift" in Chinese. We hung her pictures on the refrigerator and Gracie would tell people who visited our home, "That's Kate. She's my sister." Kate had been discovered in front of a government building—another wrapped bundle surrounded by angels waiting for her life to begin.

We bypassed the Beijing tour with the rest of our adoption group and decided to tour Shanghai this time. I thought southern cities like Dallas or Houston were hot in the summer but I felt like I'd been plopped down in a frying pan in Shanghai with the heat reflecting off the countless skyscrapers and pavement. We flew into Guangzhou on July 17, 2004, and the next day met our adoption group in the parking lot as we loaded onto the bus to get our babies. We were going to a government building where they would bring our daughters to us one by one. We walked up a couple of flights of stairs into a lobby area that was hot and humid in the Guangzhou heat. We watched as one baby after another was brought out and stepped forward when our name was called.

A woman brought Kate to me and I noticed she had her little arm shielding her face. I took her from the woman and Kate kept her arm up, burying her face into it. My heart sank recalling the baby that we'd met in Beijing on our trip to get Gracie. Kate had had an eight-hour trip in the van with the other babies and I noticed tears on her face. It had been a long day. I tried to move her arm but she'd lift it again, covering her face. Unlike Gracie who had been bathed prior to meeting us, Kate smelled institutional. I still hadn't seen her entire face and tried again to move her arm and when I did I discovered she'd been sucking on her sleeve. Her entire shoulder was wet. It was the only way she knew how to comfort herself. There were not enough arms to hold each baby in her orphanage and when Kate needed soothing or the smallest act of comfort she turned to her sleeve. Within minutes she was sound asleep sucking on her sleeve; the day was too emotional and we were too unfamiliar.

For the next three days Kate rarely cried but was timid and shy. When put down for a nap, unlike her sister, Kate always fell fast asleep, sucking on the blanket we'd brought for her. She refused solid foods and preferred her bottle. At night she fell asleep almost as soon as we put her in the crib, her blanket pressed firmly to her mouth. For several nights in a row the sucking was so loud that it woke me several times (it never woke Troy in case you're wondering). With each day that passed Kate came out of the shell she'd created to protect herself for the first ten months of her life and by the time we left China she was no longer sucking on her sleeve. She'd finally found someone to comfort her.

Kate turned eleven months old a couple of days before we headed home. She handled the long flight without any fuss; the roar of the plane helped her sleep for several hours without waking. Airport security wouldn't let me hold her as I walked through security screening but had to hold her at arm's length in front of me as if carrying hazardous material. We missed the flight into Nashville and arrived several hours later where we saw Gracie sitting atop her grandpa's shoulders at the end of a long hallway. "I see her," Gracie said, bouncing up and down. "I see her. There she is." Her sister was home.

Kate was a tender soul who would jump or cry at loud noises like the coffee grinder or vacuum. One day Gracie told her preschool teacher that *she* wasn't afraid of the coffee grinder because she knew that God was always with her. The teacher later asked me, "What kind of scary coffee grinder do you have, anyway?" If Kate climbed onto the table or bookshelves all we had to do was say, "Kate, no, no," and she would cry for several minutes. Gracie never liked to hear her sister cry and would say, "Mom! You hurt Kate's feelings." She'd then put her arm around Kate or pat her on the head. One morning as they played together in the children's area of the local mall another little girl went down the slide before Kate had a chance to get off the end and the little girl slammed right into Kate, making her cry. From across the floor I heard Gracie yell, "Hey, that's my sister!" I couldn't hear what the little girl said over Kate's wails. "You hurt my little sister," Gracie said, squaring off against her.

I ran toward them and said, "Gracie, it's okay. It was an accident."

Grace pointed to the little girl. "Mom, *she* hurt Kate and made her cry. You need to put her in time-out." I tried to explain that I had no time-out power when it came to other people's children. Gracie put her arm around Kate and led her to the huge frog in the middle of the play area and sat down on its enormous tongue, comforting her.

Gracie fell into the role of big sister with ease, becoming protector, antagonizer, and leader of playtime in one breath. One afternoon, when Kate was two and realized she didn't have to do *everything* her sister said, Gracie became aggravated with her and came to me with tears in her eyes. "Mom, let's take Kate to the zoo and sell her," she said. I convinced her that social services would frown on us for selling Kate to the zoo and within minutes the tears were gone, the zoo forgotten, and echoes of grace were once again bouncing from the walls and ceilings in singing tones.

I WAS SCHEDULED TO SPEAK in Washington in 2006, and as I prepared my notes Troy asked, "Will you talk about Kevin Taylor?" I shook my head. "Why not?" he asked.

"I just don't think anybody wants to hear about that, especially a group this big. Fourteen thousand people are scheduled for it," I said. "I think it'd work better in a smaller setting."

"I think you're wrong," he said. "Don't you think the

percentage of people at that conference who have been violated is pretty high?" I shrugged, which seemed like a perfectly good answer to me. "That's not an answer," he said. He can be so annoying at times.

On the day I was flying out I packed the girls' bags and took them to Troy's parents' house across town. I came home and threw my books, notes, and computer into my bag and realized I had thirty minutes to kill before leaving for the airport. Since my books were packed and the house was clean I turned on the television in the middle of the day, a rare feat for a parent of little ones. If the TV is on I can usually catch every tenth word or so and get so confused I would need to call a friend afterward. "What's the *one* thing Oprah said you should never eat? Is it meatballs? Because that's what we're having tonight!" I sat down and Oprah Winfrey was halfway through an interview with a young girl in Africa who had been repeatedly raped by her father. Tears streamed down the girl's face and my heart broke for her. I don't recall the exact words but Oprah said something like, "Why are you crying?" The girl couldn't answer. "Do you think this was your fault?" Oprah asked. The girl nodded and tears streamed down her face. My heart sank. God can be very pushy at times. First Troy and now Oprah! I got out my computer and began to type.

When it was time to head to the airport Troy came downstairs. "What are you doing on the computer?" he asked, anxious to leave the house.

"Changing my talk," I said.

"What do you mean? Changing it to what?"

I shut the computer and put it inside my bag, throwing it over my shoulder. "I'm talking about Kevin Taylor."

Troy grabbed a suitcase and followed after me. "What changed your mind?"

"Oprah," I said, walking out the door.

"Oprah!?" he yelled after me. "Since when do you talk to her?"

PEOPLE WERE STILL SHUFFLING IN their seats when I got up to speak but when I alluded to what happened inside the Taylor home silence fell over the arena. I didn't want it to be heavy or depressing so I interjected several humorous stories in my thirty-minute talk, and then took my seat. As I walked through the long halls toward the book-signing tables several women ran to me, sharing their own stories. An usher was guiding me toward the tables when a woman grabbed my arm. I turned and saw tears streaming down her face. "My nine-year-old daughter has recently been molested by a kid only two years older than her," she sobbed, trying to find her voice. "I don't know what to do. I don't know what to say."

"Tell her it's not her fault," I said. "Then tell her again because she won't believe you. Then tell her again because she still won't believe you. Tell her not to be ashamed. It isn't her shame. It's his. And tell her that God has not forgotten her. Tell her how much he loves her." The usher pushed me toward the tables and I never saw the woman again. I don't even know if she really heard what I said.

IN THE SPRING OF 2006, I wanted to plant more flower bulbs in a flowerbed that's beside our driveway. I got shoes on the girls and gathered my supplies and poured a bowl of fresh water for Bailey, who was now fifteen years old. The old guy didn't do as well in the heat anymore and the flowerbed I would be working in faced the pasture full of cows next to us. Whenever Bailey was outside he would sit and bark at the cows and they would moo at him. *Bark! Moo! Bark! Moo!* I never got it but it was a relationship that worked for them. I knew he'd wear himself out in the heat with all the barking but also knew he'd go crazy inside the house knowing we were outside without him, so I had decided to leave him up by the house under the shade of a big tree. I put down the water bowl and directed Bailey to sit as the girls and I made our way to the flowerbed.

I had begun to plant the bulbs when I heard barking behind me. I turned and saw Bailey sitting a few feet away barking at the cows, panting in the heat. I led him back to the shade and pointed to the clear, cold water that was just sitting there for the taking. I went back to work and within a few minutes Bailey wandered down by the flowerbed again but this time he had rambled along the fence line and had tiny cockleburs up and down his front legs. He began barking and panting again and I scolded him for the work he had created for me later because of those cockleburs. I took him back to the shade, clipped his leash to his collar, and then wrapped the other end to the watering hose so he'd think he was "stuck." I went back to work and within minutes I heard him panting and barking wildly behind me. This time the bark was frantic and I turned to see that his leash had wrapped around a small branch that had fallen during a recent storm and the end of that branch had impaled itself into the yard. "You can just sit there and bark for all I care," I said. He did just that. He barked and barked and barked till I couldn't take it anymore and I leaped up and carried him inside the house.

When I got back to the flowerbed, Gracie, who was four years old at the time and picking tiny berries off a shrub then "planting" them in the ground, said, "I know why Bailey won't stay in the shade, Mom."

I dug a hole for another bulb. "Oh yeah? Why's that?"

She never took her eyes off her work. "Because he loves you so much that he just wants to be with you."

I love you so much that I just want to be with you, the Hound of Heaven whispers. *I don't want to be tucked away at arm's length, leashed up and kept from you. I want to be with you and I'll keep coming to you again and again and again for as long as it takes.* But what do we say to him? Do we say anything at all? Do we open our hands or turn our backs? As I watched my girls run through my newly planted flowerbed I prayed that they would discover one of the greatest mysteries of the ages, that although they wouldn't know why, they *would* know that The Divine Mystery wants to be with them. I prayed that they would have open hands.

IN JULY OF THAT YEAR Troy and I submitted paperwork for another adoption. The process was now taking more than two years to adopt from China and we knew that by the time we got our child that Gracie and Kate would be two years older and we would, too. We decided to travel to

Guatemala because the wait time there was less than a year, we'd only have to be there two days as opposed to two weeks, and it was only a four-hour flight to get there. As I made dinner one afternoon I asked Gracie if she wanted God to bring her a baby brother or a baby sister. She said, "I want God to bring me a baby cow." I told her it wouldn't fit in the crib.

Other infants within the same adoption agency were coming home between five and seven months old but somehow our son's paperwork had gotten all the way to a government office called PGN then kicked back out. The director of the Guatemala program at the adoption agency called me one morning to explain that this setback could take two weeks or longer. She didn't know what was wrong or what paperwork was missing but assured me that agency workers in Guatemala were doing everything they could to help. They discovered that PGN wanted one more document signed by the woman who gave birth to our little guy. The paperwork already included four documents signed by her but for some reason, they wanted yet another signature and they didn't know how long that would take. In the meantime, infants were being united with their parents while we waited.

We used the time to paint his room a shade of blue

and wrote several boy-type quotes on the walls but on one wall we wrote the passage from Galatians that I had first heard when I was a child and had come to mean so much to me: "God had special plans for me and set me apart for his work even before I was born. He called me through his grace."

We waited three extra months for the signature issue to be resolved and in July 2007, the director finally called and said we could pick up our son. Seven days later Troy and I boarded a plane for Guatemala City to bring David Miguel home. He's named after his grandpa David; it means "beloved." At the time he was one year old and the oldest child his foster mother, Rosa, had cared for in her twelve years working in the Guatemalan foster system. The translator called us in our hotel room and said David and Rosa were in the lobby waiting for us. The elevator door opened and we recognized David immediately. He was smiling and laughing while sitting on Rosa's lap. We walked over to him and he beamed at us, reaching his arms for me. "He knows," the translator said. "He knows you're his mother." That is the beauty of adoption. My children weren't strangers in a foreign land. They were *my* children. I knew it long before I held any of them in my arms. Troy knew it long before he lifted any of them onto his shoulders. My mind knows they don't look anything like me but my heart doesn't know that. My mind knows they weren't birthed through my body but my heart doesn't know that. My mind knows that people see us and realize our children are adopted but my heart doesn't know that.

They are mine and I am theirs.

That's the deal.

WHEN THIS BOOK IS RELEASED Gracie will be in first grade and it's great fun to watch her mind expand and learn new things but like every child who starts school she'll say some things that make Troy and I say, "Where did she hear *that* from?" She came home from kindergarten one day and began playing Sleeping Beauty and Rapunzel with Kate in the kitchen. At some point the story took a wrong turn, which seemed inevitable considering they are two different stories. As it frenzied to a head I heard Gracie say, "Who cares what you think, Kate?" and Kate began to cry. I took Gracie by the hand and led her into the master bedroom.

"What did you just say to your sister?" I asked. She didn't respond. "What did you say to Kate?"

Her voice was just above a whisper. "I said, 'Who cares what you think?'"

"Were those kind words?" I asked. She didn't respond. "Were those kind words to say to your sister?" She burst into tears. I held up her chin to look at me. "What do you need to do?"

"Apologize to Kate," she blurted between sobs.

I removed the hair sticking to the tears on her face. "All right. You come back out to the kitchen when you're ready."

I went into the kitchen where Kate continued to play by herself. "Where's Grace?" she asked, missing her play-mate.

"She'll be back in a few minutes," I said.

After a while Gracie made her way into the kitchen and sat on my lap at the table where Kate was now play-ing with a puzzle. Grace was composed as she walked to the table but the moment she saw Kate and me she began crying again. She looked at Kate and blurted out some-thing indistinguishable as she sobbed. I couldn't under-stand a word she said. Kate looked at her and in one breath said, "I forgive you, Grace. What'd she say, Mom?"

Grace dispensed by a four-year-old. Kate had no idea what her sister said but it didn't matter. She had already for-given her. Grace always precedes forgiveness. God sees our downcast eyes and hobbled spirits, and as we turn our faces to him, before a word stumbles past our lips, he says, "I forgive you." But this incomprehensible forgiveness doesn't allow for what German theologian Dietrich Bonhoeffer, who lost his life to the Nazis in 1945, called "cheap grace" (careless attitude that thumbs our noses at what was given for us, prompting us to live only for ourselves). Cheap grace diminishes the power of the gift. Grace came to earth and walked among us for thirty-three years before the Romans killed him on a hill called Golgotha. There is no grace without Golgotha.

"WHY DO YOU BELIEVE IN God?" a woman asked in the corridors after another speaking engagement. It's a question all of us ask at some point but she wasn't questioning herself, she was asking me. "I feel I already know everything there is to know about God," she said, "and so I've determined that I'm an atheist." I could have said I believe in God because of Golgotha or because of the oceans or animals on the African plains but I merely made some sort of polite noise because I assumed she wanted an argument. I don't believe that God can be dissected or argued but rather experienced, and unfortunately so much of one person's "God experience" comes through the actions of another person. "In an awesome act of self-denial," British author Dorothy

Sayers said, "God entrusted his reputation to ordinary people." So often our view of God is limited to these ordinary, flesh-and-blood creatures who are poor dispensers of grace. But as I asked in an earlier chapter, the question shouldn't necessarily be why believe in God but most important, "What do I *really* think about God?"

I was recently talking to a friend who grew up in an abusive home. He's successful and bright with a beautiful family but there's a lingering wound that penetrates his conversations in the form of sarcasm and self-deprecating humor. "Don't you feel worthy of the life you live?" I asked him one afternoon.

There was no hesitation. "No," he said. "I don't."

The question rumbles in our minds, the words flowing in and out and through the maze of traffic, static on the radio, and noise from the evening news. What do you really think about God? The answer to that ultimately colors and shades every aspect of our life. *I don't think I'm worthy,* my friend says. We echo his feelings: *I don't think he loves me. I think he's cruel. I don't think he cares. I think he wants me to be miserable. I think he's uninterested. I think he's demanding. I think he's cold, angry, and distant. I think he finds me disgusting. I think he's condemning and unforgiving. I think he's weak. I think he's as disappointed in me as my parents are.*

As I began to research my writing for *The Christmas Promise* I attended several meetings of Alcoholics Anonymous. I sat in the back row as the basement room of the church in downtown Franklin filled. I stopped counting when I got to seventy-five people because I couldn't see around the poles in front of me. An African American young man came in wearing a mechanic's jumpsuit with a pick sticking out of his hair and an unlit cigarette from his mouth. He was followed by a woman wearing an expensive suit and shoes whose hair and nails were meticulous. On and on they came from all walks of life but in that room the ground was level. They weren't record-company executives, insurance agents, musicians, bank presidents, or mechanics. They were alcoholics and addicts. The meeting started and the conversation ricocheted from one person to another without an awkward pause. They all shared a common bond and the dialogue never lagged.

A middle-aged man sitting near the back introduced himself and took the floor. "I know we pray 'Thy will be done,'" he said, looking at the members around him. "But what if God's will isn't any good? I mean, what if his will isn't as good as mine?"

A petite woman in her early fifties wearing blue jeans, sneakers, and a pink cotton shirt turned around to look at him. "I'm not a religious person," she said. "But I *know* it wasn't God's will for you to be a drunk."

What do you really think about God? "I don't think his will can compare to my bondage to alcohol," *the man in AA said.* "I don't think life with him can be better than my addiction to prescription drugs. I don't think he knows what he's doing. I don't think he could ever forgive me for what I've done. I don't think he could ever love me."

"Why do you believe in God?" the woman asked me in that busy corridor.

I don't remember the answer I gave. It was probably too long and rattled in her ears. I wish I could go back and answer her again.

"Because *he* believes in me," I would say.

Isn't that enough?

AFTERWORD

IT'S WARMER IN TENNESSEE AND the banging in the attic has stopped for the day. In the middle of winter several weeks went by without any work but now the framing and Sheetrock is up, and most of the electricity and painting is finished. Troy recently brought home some hardwood flooring that came from an abandoned school that was built in the 1930s. He knows I love anything attached to a story. Troy has cleaned off the years of filth from each piece of hardwood and he and his dad are hard at work installing it. Maybe by the time this book releases I'll be pulling my chair across it to begin work on the next project.

* * *

MY OLD FRIEND PEGGY CALLED a couple of years ago to catch up. Peg is married with two children, living in Ohio, and was able to put her math skills to use as a supervisor in a bank. She has one of those dark, sick personalities who loves numbers and actually balances her checkbook every day. Really! We talked about kids and work and laughed again about Mr. TM smashing her origami. As we were finishing up our conversation she said, "Oh, did your mom tell you about the murder up here?" She mentioned the murdered woman's name but I didn't know her. "Did you ever know Kevin Taylor?"

I hadn't heard the name in years and had no idea he was still in Ohio. "He was a neighbor," I said. The Taylors lived next to us long before I knew Peggy.

"Kevin's wife came to the bank early that day," she said. "She was his second or third wife. I don't remember. She was separated from Kevin but just a day or two before she had come through the drive-through and had a sling on her arm. 'Guess who did this?' she said. She was telling everyone about it. It seemed that she was saying, 'If something happens to me. You'll know who did it.'"

"Did he kill her?" I asked.

"She came to the bank that morning," Peg said. "As she was leaving, I don't know why, but I told her to be careful."

Ironically, Kevin also visited the bank that day. He was the last customer of the day and Peggy waited on him. "There was always something about him," Peg said. "I don't know what it was but even though he was actually a good-looking man he just had this look or this sense about him that was creepy." Peggy was professional as she completed his transaction and unlocked the door for him to leave.

"They say he left the bank and went to a bar and drank till the early morning hours," she said. Kevin was the last to leave the bar in those predawn hours and went to the home he had recently shared with his wife. They argued while their only child slept in the next room. The argument escalated and Kevin's wife called the police for help. She then ran out of the house in a move the police said is instinctual for a mother in an attempt to move violence away from her child. As she ran down the road Kevin shot her in the head, killing her. He then walked into a field at the back of the house and turned the gun on himself. He was gone.

I told Troy what happened when he got home from work that afternoon. "How does that make you feel?" He asked.

"Sad," I said. I don't know anything about the middle section of Kevin's life. I don't even know about his early years. All I know are a few brief childhood years and the story of his last minutes on earth—the whole of them marked by violence. It doesn't appear that he ever knew or accepted God's love and I imagine he never experienced God's grace.

Shortly after hearing the news about Kevin my mother called and said that Randy Swann was in jail again. We had heard periodic stories over the years of his occasional jail time for sexual misconduct but this time he was in for a lengthier stay. The last I heard he was out but was on the registered sex offenders list for the state of Ohio. Another life lost to violence. I often wonder what, if anything, would have happened if I had told on either of those boys.

I recently read a book about sexual predators and one of the molesters started sexually violating children in his neighborhood when he was seven years old! At the age of seven he molested two- and three-year-olds and as he grew he continued molesting children at least five or six years younger than he. He got away with it because *none* of his victims ever said a word. He explained that in his thirty-plus years of molesting children only one child raised up against him and he left that child alone, but by then it was too late. The child ran to his parents and the sexual carnage ended in a life behind bars. He admitted that communication is one of the most effective deterrents to sexual abuse, that parents should talk to their children about appropriate behavior from adults and other children. In the book he said he marveled at the lack of communication between parents and children and how easy it was for him to molest a child.

Gracie brought home a leaflet this week from school about how a child's body is very special and needs to be treated that way. It featured several cartoon children in different "safe" and "unsafe" touching situations: a child holding hands with her friend or getting a hug from Grandma were two examples of safe touching. A child being pushed on the playground or avoiding a man hiding behind a tree were two examples of unsafe touching. In each unsafe depiction the children yelled "No! No!" or "No! I don't like that!" On one page it said if someone asks to see your private parts, which are the parts that are covered by a swimsuit, a child should say, "No! No! No! No! No! No! No!" If someone asks to touch your private parts or wants you to touch him or her on their private parts and says the touches are secret, the child should say, "No! I don't like those secrets!" I thought the leaflet was right on target and a tremendous tool for parents to help their children. I read through each page with Gracie and found myself reading with great intensity. Halfway through she said, "Mom, do you like this book? Because you're really loud." I laughed and finished the leaflet reading, "If anyone makes you feel strange or uncomfortable, run and tell an adult you can trust. If you have to, keep telling people until someone believes you."

I wondered again what would have happened if I had simply told someone about Randy Swann? Would it have stopped him from violating children and women? What if I'd run home and told my mother what Kevin did? Would that have deterred him from molesting other children or abusing women? I'll never know.

WE WELCOMED OUR FRIEND BOB Gresh last night for a couple of days while he was back in town on business. As I pulled the chicken from the oven we laughed with Bob as if time hadn't passed. Bob shook his head, looking at Troy. "It's more than twenty years and she still laughs at you," he said.

"She doesn't get out much," Troy said, grabbing David to wash his hands for dinner.

I don't know where Troy and I would be today if I hadn't opened my hands to Eternal grace. Our house would be terribly quiet and lonely without these little bodies running through it. Kate, who is as pure and virtuous as her name, tells me at least ten times a day how much she loves me. She wears me out with her constant negotiations for candy but she'll follow it up with, "I love you even when you say I can't have candy." A week or so ago she asked if she could have strawberries and I told her we didn't have any. "Okay," she said, "I guess I'll just have candy then." When I told her she couldn't have candy she said, "When I'm a mother and have a daughter named Kate, just like me, I'm going to give her *all* the candy she wants and I'm going to let her play *all* day long." My mother takes great delight in those stories.

"I had one of those children," she says. "Now you know what it's like."

Without these gifts of grace in my life I would have missed out on some of the greatest moments in history. A few weeks ago I was singing operatic style (it was loud, moving, and beautiful) when Troy sighed and said, "Would you just sing like a normal person?" Kate put her hands on her hips and said, "Dad, she is *not* a normal person. She's a *mama!*" Thank you, Kate. I sang even louder. Kate and Gracie were recently playing in the kitchen as I made dinner and Kate revealed how awesome it would be if we had a maid like Cinderella. "We don't need a maid," Gracie said to her. "We have Mom." It's always good to know one's place. Gracie used to yank off her shoes and socks and say, "Welcome home, feet!" and Kate used to hold up her little arms and say, "Hode you to me, Mama." When Gracie was four she started calling coat hangers "hooks." She would run into our closet and pull out a plastic hanger and run through the house with her "hook" at the end of her hand. The word *hook* somehow morphed into *hooker* and one day while playing imaginary Peter Pan she said to her sister, "Come on, Kate. Let's go get some more hookers for Peter Pan."

At this writing David toddles about the house and says, "Bleh," which I'm certain means, "Mom is great." He's actually content to call everything "Dog." Lucy replaced Bailey after we had to put him down in February 2007, just shy of his fifteenth birthday and although Troy despises her, David is crazy about that black, shaggy dog. Lucy was thirteen weeks old when we got her and we began to crate train her as we had done for Bailey when he was a pup. On her first morning with us I discovered Lucy had had diarrhea sometime during the night. I sprayed out the crate and gave her a bath. Troy and I repeated the process that afternoon when we returned from lunch with friends. We repeated it again the next morning, and the

next, and the next. I called the vet and asked if crate training was the best method for her.

"Oh yes," the woman at the office said. "It's the most
effective form of training because dogs won't eliminate
where they sleep."

"Really?" I said. "Because Lucy seems to be shooting
holes in that theory."

That evening Gracie called me into the living room
saying, "Mom! There's poop in here." There was a trail that
stretched from one end of the room to the other. "Here's
some," Gracie yelled from the dining room. "Here's some
more," she said from the hallway. It was the worst scavenger
hunt I'd ever been on. I took Lucy to the vet's office and left
with some meds. I took her to the vet three times in two
weeks and thought I was on the verge of losing my mind.

"She has inflammatory bowel syndrome," the vet said
on my last visit.

"IBS?" I said. "I didn't know dogs could get irritable
bowel syndrome."

"Well, technically, it's *inflammatory* bowel, not *irritable*
bowel."

I looked at him. "Regardless of the word, doesn't it mean
that the dog is pooping all over my house?" He laughed and
threw up his hands. I left the office with more medicine.

When the medicines and different food began to take effect I had to pay close attention to Lucy's signs for needing to go outside. She wouldn't bark like Bailey always did. That would have been too easy. She'd prance for two seconds and then if we didn't open the door I'd have another mess to clean. As I stepped out of the shower one morning I saw her prancing. I threw a towel around me and opened the back door where she bolted down the steps after our neighbor's cat. I flew down the steps shouting her name and she ran back to me, clamped her teeth down on the towel, and ran off again. Our neighbors had several guests eating breakfast on their side porch as Lucy romped over their property. I was equidistant from my towel and the stairs, and had to make a choice. Run for the towel and hope Lucy surrendered it, or leap for the stairs. I chose the stairs and slammed the door behind me. I couldn't look my neighbors in the eyes for several weeks after that but their cat kept coming over to visit. Sure, he said it was on the premise of finding a mole in our yard but I knew he was just there for another show.

I won personal obedience lessons in a silent auction and drove Lucy miles into the country. While driving there one hot day in August I had to borrow Troy's cousin Lindsey's car, which didn't have air-conditioning except for open windows. The back windows were childproof and only rolled down halfway. As I drove down a busy highway in Franklin, Lucy managed to jump through that half-opened window on the *way* to obedience school! *What are the odds?!* I stopped the car and darted through the slowing traffic, yelling her name. She was afraid and skittish and ran over every single lane of the highway. Horns honked and vehicles stopped as I banged together my hands and shouted, "Stay. Stay," over the noise of the engines before I finally reached her. I had recently thrown out my lower back and couldn't bend over to drag Lucy back to the car so I straddled her like a horse and walked her back.

A man in a pickup rolled down his window. "I've never seen that before," he said.

"I've never done it before," I said, shoving Lucy into the backseat again.

For all these reasons and more Troy's feelings toward Lucy were a bit harsh. After one of her bouts of IBS Troy said none too quietly that we needed to give Lucy to another family. Gracie snapped her head up and said, "But Dad, God gave Lucy to us. We can't give her to another family. We adopted her. That means she's ours forever, right?"

I saw Troy's shoulders deflate and leaned in close to his ear. "Good luck getting rid of that dog," I whispered.

We've added cats to Troy's animal woes. I never thought we'd be cat people because Troy is allergic but Gracie has always wanted one and several people said we should *get* cats to help with our mole problem. For Gracie's seventh birthday we took her and Kate to our local shelter so they could each adopt a cat. Grace named hers Cindy (short for Cinderella) and Kate named hers Katrina Kay (the first cat I've known with a middle name). Katrina has taken over the garage and the deck during the day while Cindy stays on the banks of the creek that runs behind our house. I try to point out that they're never going to catch any moles while sunning themselves on the deck and the creek bank and shoo them to the front yard where the moles are busy at work. "Come on girls," I say. "Follow me to the moles!" They just look at me and meow or clean a paw, but Lucy hasn't given up! She continues to dig to China after the moles, which pleases Troy to no end.

I SPOKE AT A BOOK club last night about *The Christmas Hope,* the third book in the Christmas Hope series. It's about a woman who hasn't celebrated Christmas in years because she has lost all reason for hope. Somewhere at the beginning of the conversation a woman asked if I was currently working on a book. I said, "Yes. It's a nonfiction book called *Finding Grace.*" The club asked questions for an hour and we talked about other books they had read or would be reading in the coming weeks. As the conversation narrowed to a close the same woman raised her hand.

"Can I ask a question about the book you're writing?" she asked. "*Finding Grace*, you said. What exactly is grace?"

"It's when you get something that you don't deserve," I said.

"What do you have to do to get it?" she asked.

"Nothing," I said.

"So it's a gift?" she asked.

"Yes."

"Do you know when it's being given to you?" she asked, leaning forward.

"Not always," one of the women in the group offered.

"You have to beware of it," another woman suggested.

"Why do you want to write that book?" the first woman asked.

"Because it's a story," I said, "and although much of the book will be my story, I hope it will remind the reader of grace or help them discover what it is."

"Huh," she said. "I never knew what grace was. I hope I can read that book."

I hope she does, too.

* * *

TROY HAS DAVID IN THE bath and the girls are fighting over who gets to stand first on the stool to brush their teeth. After intense dialogue Gracie wins. We negotiate how many books to read in bed. "Two," I say. "One each."

"Ten," Kate yells, jumping into her bed. "Ten each."

"No way. We'll be up all night."

Gracie wipes her mouth and throws the towel on the bathroom sink. "Five each, Mom," she says, running to their bookcase.

"Two each," I say, leaning back against the headboard of Kate's bed.

"Four!" Gracie yells over her shoulder.

"Three each, but they have to be short," I say. "Don't bring me the long version of *Peter Pan!*"

Kate brings me *Fuss Bunny*, which was my book as a child, and two other titles she grabs in her flurry to be first. Gracie brings me a compilation of Eloise Wilkin's stories. I replace her and Kate's names with the names in one of the stories and Gracie doubles over, laughing. "Read it again like that," she says. I read it again, and she and Kate laugh harder.

We say our prayers and I give my same speech, the one about not talking into the night. As I kiss them and walk to the door, I hear Gracie giggle. "Grace, do you have the flashlight?" I ask.

"No," she says.

"Then why are your sheets glowing?"

"Mom! How'd you see that?"

"I'm not hard of seeing," I say, lifting her sheets.

"Can I keep it? Please, Mom. I'll turn it off, I promise."

"Okay, five minutes."

"Thirty!" she says.

"Five minutes or I take it now."

She covers her head and the sheets glow in the darkness. As I walk down the stairs I hear Kate trying to whisper across the room to Gracie. "Go to sleep, Kate," I say, turning the light on at the bottom of the stairs.

"My eyes are sleeping, Mom," she yells, shaking the walls. "But my face is awake."

I scribble that down in her journal and get ready for bed. I didn't get children the way I had planned. As a matter of fact, none of my dreams turned out the way I had planned, but as my children romp through our home and I know that even tonight our girls will crawl into our bed in the wee hours of the morning, I thank God that my dreams didn't.

◆ ◆ ◆

10 THINGS YOU CAN DO IF YOU LIKED THIS BOOK

1. Simply tell a friend! Word of mouth is the most effective way to spread the word.
2. Vist www.donnavanliere.com to sign up on Donna's *Friendship List*. This keeps you up-to-date on the latest books, movies, and news from Donna.
3. Send the e-card found at www.donnavanliere.com/gracecard.html to your e-mail list. It will be an encouragement to someone.
4. Post a review on one of the online bookstores (like www.amazon.com, www.barnesandnoble.com, or www.borders.com—or all three!).
5. Read about other people's stories of *finding grace* at www.donnavanliere.com/stories.html and post your story to encourage others.
6. Buy a copy of the book for a friend—or maybe even a stranger—you never know when you will be used to help someone else *find grace!*
7. Buy a set of books and donate them to the local rescue mission, women's shelter, or hospital. Think of any place there are desperate people searching for hope and who need a touch of grace!
8. Make *Finding Grace* the next selection for any book clubs or reading groups you are a part of. Or, send a copy of the book to a group of your friends (5–10 recommended) with an invitation to a *Finding Grace* "dinner & discussion" (or "coffee & chat"). Give your friends three to four

weeks to read the book prior to the get-together and then use the discussion questions on the following page to lead a conversation about the book.

9. Are you "Web savvy"? Share how the book touched you, in your blogs; post messages in appropriate discussion groups; search and join the "Donna VanLiere Friends and Fans" group on facebook.com; or link to www.donnavanliere.com from any Web sites or e-mails you are a part of. If you aren't Web savvy, maybe e-mail your favorite appropriate Web sites to request features or info on Donna and her books.

10. Donna is a phenomenal inspirational and conference speaker. Suggest to any event organizers you may know that they book Donna for their next event or invite Donna to your next event at www.donnavanliere.com /appearance.html

R E A D I N G   G U I D E
Q U E S T I O N S*

1. Donna relates that it wasn't until she was in college and breaking up with The Boyfriend that she really comprehended grace in her life. Can you identify your first comprehension of grace? Do you know what it is?

2. Mrs. Elrick told Donna that she could "hear the language of words" but it wasn't until many years later that Donna understood what that meant. Do you feel that you've fully grasped how you've been gifted? Are you living out that gift or still journeying toward it?

3. Gertrude Stein asked on her deathbed, "What is the answer? In that case, what is the question?" Donna said the most important question she was asking at the time was "How much does the job pay and how many weeks vacation?" Are you asking your life the really important questions? What is your life trying to tell you and how are you answering?

4. Donna kept the molestation from her childhood a secret until she was an adult. How can children be taught to share these experiences? Why do you think some adult victims are unable to share?

5. Uncle Remus said, "Boy, whatever you is and wherever you is, don't be what you ain't, because when you is what you ain't, you isn't." Can you relate to this? Have you ever asked yourself the question, "What ain't you?"

6. Donna and her husband describe their path to parenthood as their greatest pain but also their greatest joy. How does pain and disappointment shape us? What would it be like if we got everything we wanted when we wanted it?

7. What is the wisdom of grace? How have you experienced grace in your own life?

8. Donna talked about wandering around in the desert of Missouri. What allowed her to continue to move forward through that period? Have you had a desert period or are you in one now? How did you get through it?

9. Many years into her struggle with infertility Donna related how she finally took her hands off the wheel of the plan she'd been driving. She also described the man in AA who said, "What if God's will isn't any good? I mean, what if it isn't as good as mine?" Why do we so often think of God's plan and dream for our life as being inept? What will it mean in your own life if you take your hands off the wheel?

*For additional reading guide questions visit www.donnavanliere.com/readingguides.html

CPSIA information can be obtained at www.ICGtesting.com
Printed in the USA
LVOW07s1134060515

437447LV00002B/2/P